baking

recipe collection

by Sainsbury's

100 delicious sweet & savoury recipes

Welcome...

...to the baking recipe collection by Sainsbury's. Inside you'll find 100 irresistible sweet and savoury recipes to give you all the baking inspiration you could wish for. From must-have classics to exciting new recipes, there's all you need to have fun and get creative in the kitchen.

Each delicious recipe has been tried, tested and tasted by Sainsbury's, so you can be sure of great results, whatever your level of baking expertise. All the dishes are made from readily available ingredients, with easy-to-follow, step-by-step instructions. The recipes are divided into clear sections, from cakes, puddings and cookies through to savoury tarts and breads, so it's easy to find just what you need. There's even a special occasions section, full of inspiring ideas for birthdays, Easter, Halloween and Christmas.

Prep and cooking times are provided, as well as nutritional information. The index at the back lists all recipes alphabetically and by main ingredient, and we've also highlighted gluten-free recipes and fun recipes that the kids can pitch in with.

You'll find everything you need for your recipes, from bakeware to exciting cake decorations, in store or at sainsburys.co.uk.

We hope you find plenty of inspiration to bake up a storm and that this book becomes an indispensable addition to your kitchen. Happy baking!

contents

Baking essentials...

Stock your storecupboard with the bare necessities and you'll be set up to bake everybody's favourites

■ Flourish with the right flour

Sainsbury's has an extensive range of flour, including organic and gluten-free lines. Stock up on these:

Plain flour, a blend of hard and soft wheat, is the most commonly used flour.

Self-raising flour has salt and baking powder already added and is generally used for making muffins and cakes.

Extra fine sponge flour, a fine, soft-wheat flour, is ideal for baked goods with a high ratio of sugar to flour and is excellent for feather-light sponge cakes and puddings with greater volume.

Bread flour is made from hard, high-protein wheat and has more gluten strength and protein content than plain or all-purpose flour, which makes it ideal for baking with yeast. Sainsbury's stocks bread flours to suit all preferences including Strong white bread flour, Strong brown bread flour, Wholemeal bread flour and Wholegrain seeded bread flour.

It's important to measure flour properly. Use too little and your cakes, biscuits and bread will collapse when you take them out of the oven. Use too much, and they'll be tough and dry. Store flour in a sealed container in a cool, dry place for up to 6 months.

■ Quality ingredients are the key to success

Sugar
You can use granulated sugar when baking, but caster sugar dissolves more easily and gives a finer texture.
Brown sugar is less sweet than white sugar, because the molasses that flavour it are rather bitter. The light and dark brown varieties are interchangeable depending on the desired amount of molasses flavour.
Demerara sugar is ideal for baking, as it won't melt in the heat of the oven. It also adds a delicious crunch to the surface of muffins, biscuits, scones and bread & butter pudding (see page 72).
Muscovado sugar is rich, dark and moist. It has a hint of butterscotch, which makes it fantastic in a caramel tart (see page 88).

Eggs
All Sainsbury's eggs come from cage-free hens. Remove eggs from the fridge about 2 hours before use to prevent them from curdling.

Butter
If you want butter at room temperature, remove from the fridge 1 hour before use.

Baking powder
The powder in this raising agent is activated when liquid is added, so aim to get your cake mixture into the oven quickly once the wet ingredients have been mixed into the dry ingredients.

Bicarbonate of soda
Commonly referred to as 'bicarb' or baking soda, this is not interchangeable with baking powder, even though they are sometimes used together. Bicarb is especially good in recipes for soda bread and gingerbread.

Yeast
Dried yeast can become inactive if it's kept for too long. If it doesn't froth up to a good foamy head, it's probably stale and won't raise the dough mixture. Once the packet is open, use within 2 months. Use a fast-action yeast for quicker home-baking.

Vanilla extract
This adds a sweet depth of flavour to baked goodies.

Kit yourself out

For the best baking results, you need the right tools. Sainsbury's has an array of fantastic bakeware to help you create, decorate and display your baking masterpieces. The proof is in the pudding...

3-tier cake stands
Show off your cupcakes on a handy disposable stand

Porcelain cake stand
Let cakes, meringues and tarts take centre stage

Set of 2 kids' cake tins
The kids can store their little cakes in these tins

Fluted silicone cases
These colourful cases are ideal for baking fairy cakes

Silicone utensils
Spatula spoon, pastry brush and whisk, from a selection

Springform cake tin
The loose base lets you get the cake out the right way up

Crinkle-edged cutters
Ideal for making biscuits and cookies

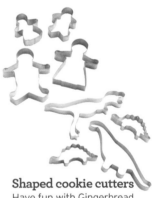

Shaped cookie cutters
Have fun with Gingerbread family or Dinosaur cutters

Cook's Collection 2lb loaf tin
With a quality non-stick finish

Cake tin liners
These pre-cut liners are ideal for large cakes

Sandwich tin
The perfect tin for shallow cakes

Silicone bakeware
Easy-release silicone bakeware, from a selection

From dainty cupcake frills and pretty cake tins to durable bakeware and utensils, all your baking needs are covered

Measuring cups
Great for measuring flour, sugar and liquids

Mini loaf cake cases
These clever cases will shape mini loaves perfectly

Wire rack/muffin tin
Two essentials for creating fabulous muffins

Mixing bowl
Whip up delicious treats in a large, stainless-steel bowl

Cupcake frills
Dress your cupcakes up in these decorative frills

Silicone cake cases
Available in a selection of sizes and colours

Ceramic baking beans
These help prevent your pastry shrinking as it cooks

Useful utensils
Palette knife, rolling pin and whisk, from a selection

Patterned paper cases
Coloured paper cases give cupcakes a party finish

Fluted flan/tartlet tins
Great for quiches, flans and tarts, large and small

Disposable piping bags
These fit any nozzle to help you decorate cakes galore

Mini pudding moulds
The perfect size for individual sponge puds

cakes

Serves 8
Prep time: 15 minutes,
plus cooling time
Cook time: 25 minutes

Classic Victoria sponge

Two light sponge cakes sandwiched with jam and dusted with icing sugar – an all-time family favourite

---

½ teaspoon oil, for greasing
170g unsalted butter
170g caster sugar
4 medium eggs, lightly beaten

170g self-raising flour, sifted
3 tablespoons raspberry jam
1 teaspoon icing sugar, for dusting

---

1 Preheat the oven to 180°C, fan 160°C, gas 4. Grease 2 x 18cm round cake tins with oil, then line the base of each with baking parchment.

2 Cream the butter and sugar together until light and fluffy. Gradually add the eggs, a little at a time, beating well between each addition. Fold in the flour and add 3 tablespoons water to bring the mixture to a dropping consistency.

3 Divide the mixture between the 2 tins and bake on the middle shelf for 25 minutes, until well risen and golden.

4 Leave the cakes to cool slightly in their tins, then remove the base liners and transfer to a wire rack to cool completely.

5 Sandwich the cakes together with the jam and dust the top with icing sugar.

Per serving: 379 cals, 21g fat, 12.8g sat fat, 26.3g total sugars, 0.3g salt

---

Did you know...?
Sainsbury's was the first major supermarket to source all its whole eggs from cage-free hens, improving the lives of 800,000 birds

'Everyone will love this deliciously light, classic Victoria sponge'

Serves 12
Prep time: 20 minutes,
plus cooling time
Cook time: 1 hour

Victoria sandwich loaf

with strawberries & cream filling

Layering a Victoria sandwich with thick cream, sweet summer strawberries and tangy lemon curd makes this classic even better

225g unsalted butter, at room temperature, plus extra for greasing
225g caster sugar
4 medium eggs, beaten
225g self-raising flour

FOR THE FILLING
1 x 300ml pot Sainsbury's double cream
5 tablespoons lemon curd
200g strawberries, hulled and quartered
icing sugar, for dusting

1 Preheat the oven to 180°C, fan 160°C, gas 4. Grease a 2lb loaf tin and line with baking parchment.

2 Cream the butter and sugar together with an electric hand mixer, until pale and fluffy. Add the eggs very gradually, beating all the time. If the mixture curdles, add a little of the flour.

3 From a height, sift in the flour and fold in using a metal spoon. Pour the mixture into the loaf tin and bake on the middle shelf of the oven for about 1 hour, until risen and golden, or until a skewer inserted into the cake comes out clean. Allow to cool in the tin for 30 minutes, then transfer to a wire rack to cool completely.

4 To make the filling, whip the cream until soft but not too stiff (don't whip for too long as the lemon curd will thicken the cream even more). Briefly fold 3 tablespoons lemon curd into the cream to get a marbled effect.

5 Cut the cake into 3 layers using a serrated bread knife. Gently heat the remaining 2 tablespoons lemon curd. Spread half the cream over the bottom layer, drizzle with the lemon curd and add half the strawberries. Top with the middle layer, then add the remaining cream, strawberries and lemon curd. Add the top layer. Dust with icing sugar and serve as soon as possible.

Per serving: 448 cals, 30.6g fat, 18.4g sat fat, 25g total sugars, 0.3g salt

Strawberries and cream are the perfect match for a Victoria sandwich

Serves 12
Prep time: 20 minutes,
plus chilling time
Cook time: 30 minutes

Pomegranate, cranberry & white chocolate cake

This striking cake would also make a delicious alternative to Christmas cake

200g unsalted butter, softened
200g caster sugar
1 teaspoon ground cinnamon
4 medium eggs
200g self-raising flour
½ x 200g pack Sainsbury's ground almonds
1 teaspoon baking powder
100g dried, sweetened cranberries, chopped
2 tablespoons semi-skimmed milk

TO DECORATE
2 x 200g bars Sainsbury's Belgian white chocolate, broken up
1 x 300ml pot Sainsbury's double cream
3 tablespoons fresh pomegranate seeds
1 tablespoon white chocolate curls, shaved from a chocolate bar with a vegetable peeler
1 tablespoon icing sugar

1 Preheat the oven to 180°C, fan 160°C, gas 4. Line 2 x 20cm round cake tins with baking parchment.

2 Beat the butter, sugar and cinnamon until light and creamy. Add the eggs, one at a time, beating well after each addition. Beat in the flour, almonds and baking powder, then stir in the cranberries and milk.

3 Divide the mixture between the 2 tins, then level. Bake for 30 minutes, until golden and beginning to shrink from the sides of the tin. Cool on a wire rack.

4 Meanwhile, make the icing. Place the chocolate in a medium bowl. Pour the cream into a pan and bring to a simmer over a low heat. Pour over the chocolate, stirring to melt in the residual heat. When melted, cool slightly then chill in the fridge for 1½ hours, until the mixture is cold and has a thick, spreading consistency. Whip with an electric hand mixer until light and fluffy.

5 Sandwich the 2 cakes together with some of the icing, then cover the whole cake with the remaining icing, creating texture with a palette knife. Sprinkle over the pomegranate seeds and chocolate curls and sift on the icing sugar.

Per serving: 669 cals, 44.3g fat, 24.5g sat fat, 46.2 total sugars, 0.4g salt

Serves 14
Prep time: 25 minutes,
plus cooling time
Cook time: 1 hour

Carrot & apple loaf

with cream cheese frosting

Grated carrot and apple make this cake extra moist and moreish

350g plain flour
2 teaspoons baking powder
1 teaspoon ground cinnamon
½ teaspoon bicarbonate of soda
½ teaspoon salt
200g light brown soft sugar
4 Sainsbury's free-range Woodland medium eggs
130ml vegetable oil, plus extra for greasing
2 medium carrots, grated (about 150g)

1 medium apple, peeled, cored and grated (about 160g)

FOR THE FROSTING
100g unsalted butter, at room temperature
150g soft cheese, at room temperature
300g icing sugar
1 teaspoon vanilla extract
Fiddes Payne pearl swirls, to decorate

1 Preheat the oven to 180°C, fan 160°C, gas 4. Lightly grease a 2lb loaf tin and line with baking parchment.

2 In a bowl, combine the flour, baking powder, cinnamon, bicarbonate of soda and salt. In another large bowl, whisk together the sugar and eggs, then add the oil. Stir in the carrot and apple.

3 Add the dry mixture to the wet, stirring until just blended. Pour into the prepared loaf tin and level the top. Bake for 1 hour, or until a skewer inserted into the cake comes out clean. Leave to cool in the tin for 30 minutes, then transfer to a wire rack to cool completely before icing.

4 For the frosting, use an electric hand mixer on a medium speed to beat the butter until smooth. Add the soft cheese and continue to beat. Reduce the speed of the mixer to low, add the icing sugar and vanilla extract, then continue to beat until the mixture is fluffy.

5 Cut the cake horizontally into 3 layers. Sandwich together with some of the frosting and smooth the rest over the top. Decorate with the pearl swirls.

Per serving: 439 cals, 20g fat, 7.6g sat fat, 39.2g total sugars, 0.6g salt

Serves 12
Prep time: 25 minutes,
plus cooling time
Cook time: 25 minutes

Classic chocolate cake

This impressive, light and airy chocolate cake is surprisingly easy to make

2 x 18cm Sainsbury's cake tin liners
200g unsalted butter, softened
200g Sainsbury's Fairtrade caster sugar
3 medium eggs, beaten
200g Taste the Difference extra fine sponge flour, sifted
60g Sainsbury's Fairtrade cocoa powder, sifted

2 tablespoons semi-skimmed milk

TO DECORATE
150g unsalted butter or margarine, softened
300g icing sugar, sifted
60g Sainsbury's Fairtrade cocoa powder, sifted
Sainsbury's sugar stars

1 Preheat the oven to 180°C, fan 160°C, gas 4. Line 2 x 18cm round cake tins with the cake tin liners – these will give the cake edges an attractive texture.

2 In a large mixing bowl, beat together the butter and sugar, until light and creamy. Add the eggs, a little at a time, beating well after each addition. Add a little flour if the mixture starts to curdle.

3 Add the flour, cocoa powder and milk and beat until smooth. Divide the mixture between the 2 tins and bake on the middle shelf of the oven for 25 minutes, until well risen. Remove from the oven, lift the cakes out onto a wire rack and leave to cool completely in the liners.

4 Meanwhile, make the icing. Using an electric hand mixer, beat the butter or margarine in a large bowl until fluffy. Add the icing sugar and cocoa powder and continue to beat until smooth and creamy. As the mixture becomes a little dry, add 3 tablespoons boiling water and mix well.

5 Sandwich the 2 cakes together with half the icing. Spread the remaining icing on top of the cake and create peaks, using the back of a spoon, before it sets, as this will help prevent the decorations from rolling off. Sprinkle with the sugar stars.

Per serving: 507 cals, 28g fat, 17.3g sat fat, 44.8g total sugars, 0.4g salt

'Cake tin liners lend a professional finish to this rich chocolate cake'

Marble cake

Serves 10
Prep time: 20 minutes, plus cooling time
Cook time: 45 minutes

One fantastic marble cake recipe, two great ways to serve it

225g unsalted butter, softened, plus extra for greasing
225g caster sugar
4 medium eggs
225g self-raising flour, plus extra for dusting
1 teaspoon vanilla extract

100ml milk, plus 1 tablespoon extra
3 tablespoons cocoa powder
1 tablespoon golden syrup
60g caster sugar
100g dark chocolate, broken up
Sainsbury's chocolate crispies, to decorate

1 Preheat the oven to 180°C, fan 160°C, gas 4. Beat the butter with the sugar until light and creamy. Add the eggs, one at a time, mixing well. Mix in the flour, vanilla and 100ml milk until smooth. Spoon half the mixture into another bowl and stir in the cocoa and 1 tablespoon milk.

2 Grease a 20cm cake tin and dust with flour. Place alternate spoonfuls of each mixture into the cake tin. Drag through a skewer to create a marbled effect. Bake for 30 minutes, then cover with foil and bake for a further 10–15 minutes, or until a skewer inserted comes out clean. Leave to cool.

3 For the ganache, heat the syrup, sugar and 2 tablespoons water in a pan, stirring. Bring to the boil, then remove from the heat. Add the chocolate. Leave to melt, then stir until glossy. Spread on the cake and top with the crispies.

Per serving: 481 cals, 26g fat, 16.2g sat fat, 37.5g total sugars, 0.4g salt

Marble cupcakes

Follow step 1 above. Spoon both mixtures into a greased 12-hole muffin tin. Create a marbled effect (see step 2, above) and bake for 25–30 minutes, until a skewer inserted comes out clean. For the buttercream, beat 250g unsalted butter, 150g icing sugar and 1 teaspoon vanilla extract with an electric whisk, until creamy. Pipe onto the cooled cakes using a piping bag. Top with Sainsbury's mini honeycomb pieces and wrap in Sainsbury's cupcake frills.

SERVES 12 Prep time: 10 minutes Cook time: 30 minutes

Each: 539 cals, 35.9g fat, 22.3g sat fat, 34.7g total sugars, 0.3g salt

Apple cake

This gorgeous cake is also great served warm for dessert

Serves 8
Prep time: 25 minutes, plus cooling time
Cook time: 1 hour, 15 minutes

225g self-raising flour
1 teaspoon baking powder
170g caster sugar
115g butter, melted, plus extra for greasing
1 teaspoon Taste the Difference French almond extract

2 medium eggs
400g Braeburn apples, peeled, cored and each chopped into 8
25g flaked almonds
2 tablespoons apricot jam, warmed

1 Preheat the oven to 160°C, fan 140°C, gas 3. Grease a 20cm round cake tin and line the base with baking parchment.

2 Place the flour, baking powder and sugar in a medium bowl. Add the melted butter, almond extract and eggs, one at a time, beating well after each addition.

3 Place half the mixture in the cake tin and top with the apples. Blob over the remaining mixture, leaving apples poking through. Sprinkle with the almonds.

4 Bake for about 1 hour, 15 minutes, or until the cake is golden, firm to the touch and slightly shrunk from the sides of the tin. Cool in the tin for 15 minutes, then remove and brush with the jam. Great served with single cream.

Per serving: 377 cals, 16.5g fat, 9.6g sat fat, 30.9g total sugars, 0.4g salt

Tea cake

Place 350g dried mixed fruit in a bowl and cover with 350ml black tea made with 1 Red Label tea bag. Cover and leave to soak overnight, then mix with 2 beaten eggs, 270g self-raising flour, 200g dark brown soft sugar and 1 teaspoon ground cinnamon. Bake in a preheated oven at 180°C, fan 160°C, gas 4 for 1½ hours. Cool on a wire rack, then slice and serve with butter for a rich afternoon tea treat.

SERVES 12 Prep time: 10 minutes, plus overnight soaking
Cook time: 1½ hours

Slice: 238 cals, 1.5g fat, trace sat fat, 36.1g total sugars, 0.2g salt

Serves 10
Prep time: 20 minutes
Cook time: 45 minutes

Lemon & blueberry polenta cake

This deliciously light, wheat-free cake is made with polenta instead of flour, which helps keep the berries suspended as it cooks – perfect for gluten-free diets

100g unsalted butter, plus extra for greasing
100g caster sugar
2 medium eggs, beaten
½ x 200g pack Sainsbury's ground almonds
90g polenta

zest and juice of 1 lemon
1 teaspoon baking powder
100ml natural yogurt
100g blueberries

1 Preheat the oven to 180°C, fan 160°C, gas 4. Grease a 2lb loaf tin and line with baking parchment.

2 Using an electric hand mixer, cream the butter and sugar together in a bowl until soft and pale. Beat in the eggs, one at a time, adding 1 tablespoon ground almonds with each egg.

3 Stir through the polenta, lemon juice and zest, baking powder and remaining ground almonds, then stir in the yogurt and half the blueberries.

4 Pour into the loaf tin and scatter the remaining blueberries over the top, lightly pressing into the mixture. Bake for 45 minutes, or until a skewer inserted into the centre comes out clean.

Per serving: 242 cals, 15.3g fat, 6.6g sat fat, 12.5g total sugars, 0.2g salt

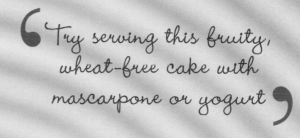

Serves 8
Prep time: 15 minutes,
plus simmering
and cooling time
Cook time: 1 hour

Orange pudding cake

This zingy citrus cake has a beautifully moist and pudding-like texture

oil, for greasing
2 medium oranges, washed
5 medium eggs
225g caster sugar
1 x 200g pack Sainsbury's ground almonds

50g plain flour
1 teaspoon baking powder
1 tablespoon icing sugar, for dusting
zest of 1 orange, to decorate

1 Preheat the oven to 180°C, fan 160°C, gas 4. Grease a 20cm round springform cake tin and line with baking parchment.

2 Place the oranges, whole and unpeeled, in a saucepan and cover with water. Place on the hob, bring to the boil, then simmer for 1 hour. Remove the oranges and whizz, including the peel, in a food processor.

3 Add the eggs, caster sugar, almonds, flour and baking powder to the food processor and whizz with the oranges until just blended.

4 Pour into the cake tin and bake in the oven for 1 hour, until a skewer inserted into the middle of the cake comes out clean. Cool in the tin.

5 Remove from the tin. Dust the top of the cake with icing sugar, then sprinkle with orange zest. Great served with mascarpone.

Per serving: 379 cals, 18.1g fat, 2.7g sat fat, 35.4g total sugars, 0.3g salt

Did you know...?
Sainsbury's sources all its own-brand sugar from Fairtrade producers. This generates money in Fairtrade premium for communities in Malawi and Zambia to fund community projects

Serves 8
Prep time: 15 minutes,
plus cooling time
Cook time: 25 minutes

Chocolate roulade
with white chocolate frosting

Fulfil your chocolate cravings with a slice of rich roulade. Made without flour, it's the ideal treat for friends and family following a gluten-free diet

oil for greasing
170g Sainsbury's Belgian dark chocolate, broken up
5 Sainsbury's free-range Woodland medium eggs, separated

225g golden caster sugar
200ml double cream
1 teaspoon vanilla extract
1 tablespoon icing sugar, sifted
80g white chocolate, broken up

1 Preheat the oven to 200°C, fan 180°C, gas 6. Grease a 33 x 23cm swiss roll tin and line with baking parchment.

2 Melt the dark chocolate in a bowl over a pan of just-simmering water, making sure the bowl doesn't touch the water. Stir until smooth, then set aside.

3 In a large, clean bowl, whisk together the egg yolks and all but 1 tablespoon of the caster sugar, until pale and thick. Mix in the melted chocolate and 1 tablespoon hot water, until smooth.

4 In another clean bowl, whisk the egg whites until stiff, then whisk in the remaining 1 tablespoon caster sugar. Lightly fold into the chocolate mixture using a large metal spoon, then spoon into the prepared tin. Bake for 15-20 minutes, until risen and springy to the touch.

5 Cover with a sheet of baking parchment and a damp tea towel. Leave for 15 minutes. Remove the tea towel and leave to stand until completely cold.

6 In a bowl, whip the cream, vanilla extract and icing sugar until soft peaks are formed. Remove the parchment and turn out the roulade onto a clean sheet of parchment. Spread with the cream to within 2cm of the edge. With the long side towards you, and using the paper to help, roll up the roulade.

7 Melt the white chocolate as in step 2. Using a teaspoon, drizzle the melted chocolate all over the roulade. Cut into slices to serve.

Per serving: 458 cals, 27.8g fat, 15.8g sat fat, 41.2g total sugars, 0.2g salt

Traditional ginger cake

Ground and stem ginger give this beautifully moist cake a delightful flavour

Serves 10
Prep time: 30 minutes, plus cooling time
Cook time: 45 minutes

225g self-raising flour
2 teaspoons ground ginger
½ teaspoon ground cinnamon
1 teaspoon bicarbonate of soda
100g unsalted butter, plus extra for greasing
100g golden syrup
100g black treacle

100g light brown soft sugar
50g stem ginger, diced, plus 2 tablespoons ginger syrup (from the jar)
2 Sainsbury's free-range Woodland medium eggs
200ml semi-skimmed milk
100g icing sugar

1 Preheat the oven to 180°C, fan 160°C, gas 4. Grease a 20cm square cake tin and line with baking parchment.

2 In a food processor, whizz together the flour, ginger, cinnamon, bicarbonate of soda and butter until it resembles fine breadcrumbs.

3 Place the golden syrup, black treacle, light brown sugar and diced stem ginger in a pan. Heat gently until all the sugar has dissolved, then cook for another minute over a high heat and remove.

4 Beat the eggs and milk into the syrup mixture, then mix into the flour and butter mixture. Pour into the cake tin and bake for 45 minutes.

5 Meanwhile, stir the ginger syrup and 2 tablespoons boiling water into the icing sugar until smooth. Remove the cake from the oven and allow it to cool for 10 minutes, then pierce all over with a skewer. Pour over the icing sugar mixture and leave to set before serving.

Per serving: 337 cals, 10.1g fat, 5.5g sat fat, 39.5g total sugars, 0.7g salt

Did you know...?
Sainsbury's was the first major supermarket to source all its whole eggs from cage-free hens, improving the lives of 800,000 birds

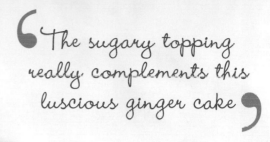

Serves 12
Prep time: 20 minutes,
plus cooling time
Cook time: 40 minutes

Flourless chocolate torte

Made with ground almonds instead of flour, this gorgeous torte is perfect
if you're following a gluten-free diet

2 x 100g bars Taste the Difference Santo
Domingo organic dark chocolate, broken up
200g unsalted butter, plus extra for greasing
1 teaspoon vanilla extract
5 medium eggs, separated

150g Sainsbury's Fairtrade caster sugar
½ x 200g pack Sainsbury's ground almonds
50g Sainsbury's Fairtrade cocoa powder,
sifted
icing sugar, for dusting

1 Preheat the oven to 180°C, fan 160°C, gas 4. Grease a 25cm round
   springform cake tin.

2 Melt the chocolate and butter together in the microwave on high for
   1–3 minutes, depending on your microwave, or melt over a pan of simmering
   water on the hob. Stir in the vanilla extract.

3 Beat the egg yolks with 50g caster sugar until pale in colour, then pour in
   the chocolate mixture. Fold in the almonds and cocoa powder.

4 Beat the egg whites until stiff, then gradually add the remaining 100g
   caster sugar until combined. Fold one-third of the egg white into the
   chocolate mixture, then gently fold in the rest until just blended.

5 Spoon into the tin, spreading evenly, and bake for 30–35 minutes. Let the
   cake stand for 10 minutes before dusting with icing sugar.

Per serving: 372 cals, 27.3g fat, 14.2g sat fat, 22.7g total sugars, 0.2g salt

Serving suggestion
This torte is delicious served with whipped
mascarpone cheese sweetened with icing sugar

Serves 8
Prep time: 20 minutes,
plus cooling time
Cook time: 12 minutes

Lemon curd & almond swiss roll

The sweet sponge is the perfect foil for the citrus kick of the lemon curd

3 large eggs
85g caster sugar, plus extra for sprinkling
zest of 1 lemon

85g plain flour
4 tablespoons lemon curd
40g Sainsbury's toasted flaked almonds

1 Preheat the oven to 190°C, fan 170°C, gas 5. Line a 33 x 23cm swiss roll tin with baking parchment.

2 Using an electric hand mixer, beat the eggs and sugar together for about 5 minutes, until the mixture is very pale in colour and the whisks leave a trail. Fold in the lemon zest and 1 tablespoon warm water, then sift in the flour, a third at a time, folding it gently into the egg mixture using a large spoon.

3 Pour the mixture into the prepared tin, spread it evenly and bake in the oven for 10-12 minutes, or until the centre springs back when touched.

4 Meanwhile, place a piece of baking parchment on the work surface and sprinkle liberally with sugar. Take the sponge out of the oven and invert it onto the sugared paper. Remove the tin and carefully peel away the baking parchment tin liner. Trim the edges. Score 1cm in from the edge all the way along one of the shortest sides, so the sponge tucks inwards easily. Roll up the sponge with the sugared paper inside, then leave to cool.

5 Once cold, unroll and spread with the lemon curd. Roll up the sponge into a swiss roll shape (use the sugared paper to help you). Sprinkle with the almonds.

Per serving: 193 cals, 7.7g fat, 2.5g sat fat, 16.5g total sugars, 0.2g salt

Serves 12
Prep time: 20 minutes,
plus cooling time
Cook time: 1 hour

Banana loaf

Dark chocolate adds a tasty twist to this popular cake

175g plain flour
2 teaspoons baking powder
½ teaspoon bicarbonate of soda
125g unsalted butter, melted, plus extra for greasing
150g Sainsbury's Fairtrade golden caster sugar
2 large eggs
1 teaspoon vanilla extract

275g very ripe banana (weighed without skin, approx 3 small bananas), mashed
150g dark chocolate, cut into ½ cm chunks

TO DECORATE
100g icing sugar
20g dark chocolate, roughly chopped
½ x 100g pack Sainsbury's banana coins

1 Preheat the oven to 180°C, fan 160°C, gas 4. Grease a 2lb loaf tin and line with baking parchment.

2 In a bowl, mix together the flour, baking powder and bicarbonate of soda.

3 In a large bowl, beat together the melted butter and caster sugar until blended. Beat in the eggs one at a time, then beat in the vanilla extract and banana.

4 Gradually add the flour mixture, mixing well after each addition, then stir through the chopped chocolate. Pour into the loaf tin and bake on the middle shelf of the oven for 50 minutes to 1 hour. When it's cooked a skewer inserted into the centre should come out clean. Leave in the tin to cool.

5 Mix the icing sugar with 4 teaspoons water to form a paste. Remove the cake from the tin and drizzle over the icing. Decorate with the chopped chocolate and banana coins.

Per serving: 358 cals, 16g fat, 8.9g sat fat, 34.5g total sugars, 0.4g salt

Did you know...?
Sainsbury's was the first supermarket to convert its entire banana range to 100% Fairtrade, and now sells more Fairtrade bananas than all the other major UK supermarkets combined

Serves 8
Prep time: 15 minutes,
plus cooling time
Cook time: 25 minutes

Coffee & walnut cake

This classic cake is a perfect addition to afternoon tea

2 tablespoons instant coffee granules
200g unsalted butter, plus extra for greasing
200g Sainsbury's Fairtrade golden caster sugar
4 medium eggs
200g self-raising flour
1 teaspoon baking powder

1 x 100g pack Sainsbury's walnut halves, roughly chopped

FOR THE BUTTERCREAM ICING
2 teaspoons instant coffee granules
150g unsalted butter
300g icing sugar, sifted

1 Preheat the oven to 180°C, fan 160°C, gas 4. Grease 2 x 20cm round cake tins and line with baking parchment. Dissolve the coffee granules in 1 tablespoon boiling water and allow to cool.

2 Beat together the butter and sugar until light and fluffy, then add the eggs, one at a time, beating well after each addition. Using a large spoon, fold in the flour and baking powder. Stir in 50g walnuts and the coffee.

3 Divide the mixture between the 2 cake tins and bake for 20-25 minutes, until golden and springy to the touch. Remove the cakes from the tins and leave to cool on a wire rack.

4 To make the icing, dissolve the coffee granules in 1 teaspoon boiling water. Beat together the butter and icing sugar until pale and fluffy. Stir in the coffee and mix until well combined. Use half the buttercream icing to sandwich the cakes together. Cover the top with the remaining icing and decorate with the remaining walnuts.

Per serving: 807 cals, 47.8g fat, 26.1g sat fat, 65.8g total sugars, 0.5g salt

“Crunchy walnuts complement the rich coffee buttercream”

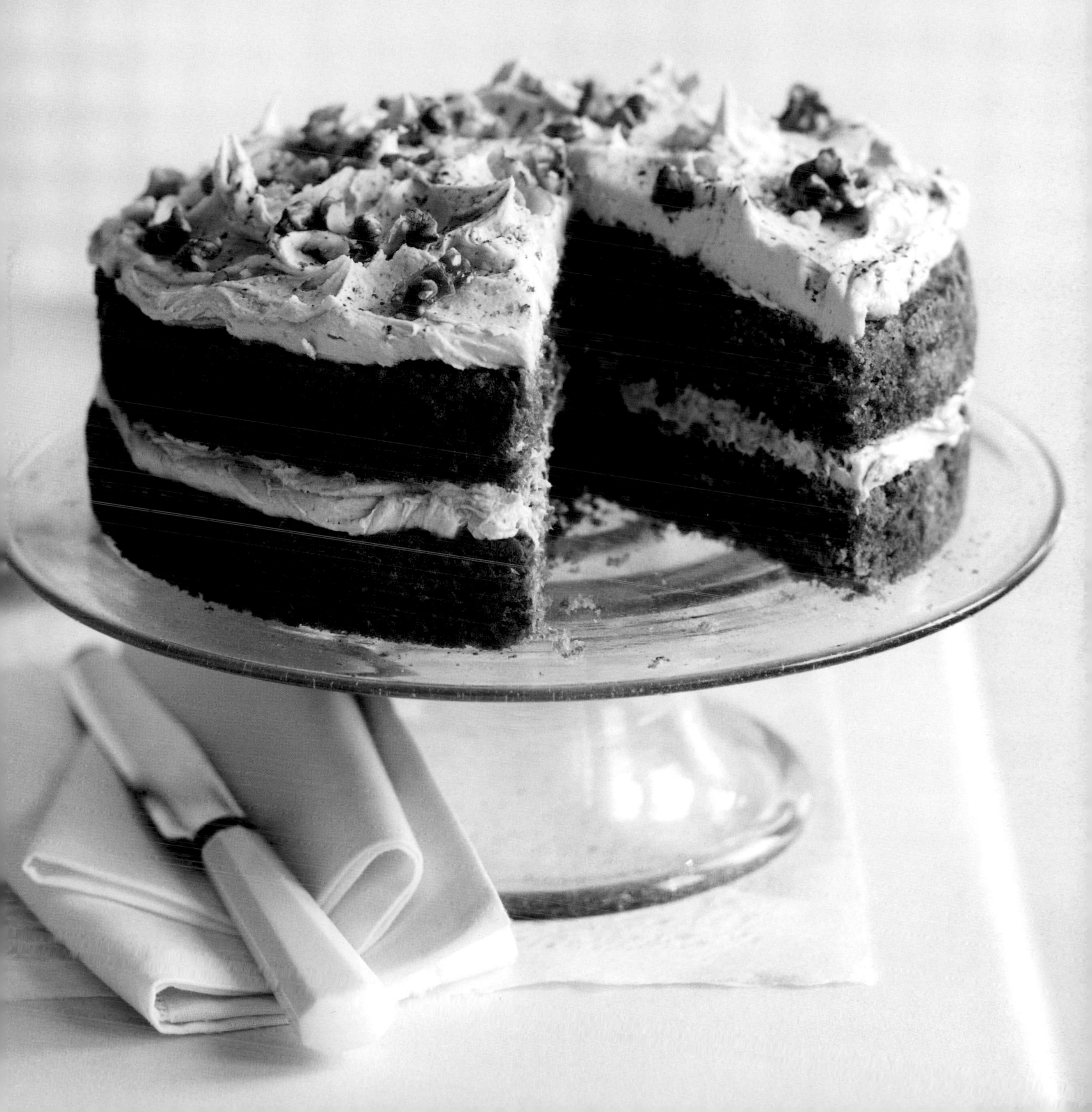

cupcakes, muffins & more

Makes 9
Prep time: 20 minutes,
plus cooling time
Cook time: 50 minutes

Rhubarb cakes

The zingy flavours of rhubarb and ginger make a mouthwatering combination

300g rhubarb
juice of ½ a lemon
165g self-raising flour
175g butter, softened, plus extra for greasing
175g caster sugar
3 large eggs
2 teaspoons vanilla extract

FOR THE TOPPING
25g unsalted butter
2 tablespoons self-raising flour
1 tablespoon caster sugar
2 teaspoons ground ginger
icing sugar, to dust
crème fraîche and honey, to serve

1 Preheat the oven to 180°C, fan 160°C, gas 4. Grease a 23cm square cake tin and line with baking parchment.

2 Trim the rhubarb and chop into 3cm pieces. Place in a bowl with the lemon juice. In a separate bowl, beat together the flour, butter, sugar, eggs and vanilla extract. Fold in half the rhubarb and spoon the mixture into the bottom of the tin, spreading it out with a spatula. Scatter over the remaining rhubarb.

3 For the topping, rub the butter into the flour, then stir in the sugar and ginger. Sprinkle over the cake mixture and bake for 40–50 minutes. Leave to cool for 10 minutes, then remove from the tin. Dust with icing sugar, then slice into squares. Serve warm or cold with crème fraîche, drizzled with honey.

Per serving: 364 cals, 21g fat, 12.2g sat fat, 22.8g total sugars, 0.3g salt

Plum & almond muffins

Preheat the oven to 180°C, fan 160°C, gas 4. Line a 12-hole muffin tin with cases. In a bowl, whisk 3 large eggs with 150g caster sugar. Stir in 25g unsalted butter, melted, then fold in 175g self-raising flour, 25g ground almonds and 3 stoned, finely chopped plums (don't over-mix). Spoon into the muffin cases. Scatter with 2 tablespoons flaked almonds and bake for 20–25 minutes, then cool on a wire rack.

MAKES 12   Prep time: 15 minutes   Cook time: 25 minutes

Each: 178 cals, 6.3g fat, 1.9g sat fat, 14.7g total sugars, 0.2g salt

Makes 12
Prep time: 10 minutes,
plus cooling time
Cook time: 25 minutes

Bursting berry muffins

These easy-to-make muffins are full of fresh, fruity flavours

340g plain flour
1 teaspoon baking powder
225g caster sugar
120g unsalted butter, melted and cooled

2 medium eggs, beaten
½ x 500g pot Sainsbury's natural yogurt
1 x 150g pack Sainsbury's blackberries
150g blueberries

1 Preheat the oven to 200°C, fan 180°C, gas 6. Line a 12-hole muffin tin with cases.

2 Sift the flour and baking powder into a large bowl. Stir in the sugar.

3 In a separate bowl combine the butter with the eggs and yogurt.

4 Lightly stir the liquid mixture into the flour mixture, gradually incorporating all the flour. Stir in the blackberries and blueberries. Spoon the mixture into the muffin cases, filling nearly to the top, then bake in the oven for 25 minutes.

5 Transfer to a wire rack and leave to cool.

Per serving: 296 cals, 9.9g fat, 5.6g sat fat, 23.2g total sugars, 0.1g salt

Lemon cakes

Preheat the oven to 180°C, fan 160°C, gas 4. Mix together 150g unsalted butter, melted, 150g plain flour, 150g light brown soft sugar, 2 eggs, beaten, and 4 teaspoons Taste the Difference Sicilian lemon extract. Pour into 8 Sainsbury's mini loaf cake cases and bake for 25 minutes. Cool slightly, then remove the cases. Mix 100g caster sugar with 200g icing sugar, 50ml cold water and 3 teaspoons lemon extract. Pour over the warm cakes, and scatter with lemon zest.

MAKES 8   Prep time: 10 minutes   Cook time: 25 minutes

Each: 461 cals, 17.2g fat, 10.8g sat fat, 57.9g total sugars, trace salt

Packed with berries, these fab muffins are impossible to resist

Makes 10
Prep time: 15 minutes
Cook time: 20 minutes

Honey & raisin muffins

These healthier muffins would be great for breakfast - zap them in the microwave for 20 seconds on high to get that fresh-out-of-the-oven taste

180g self-raising flour
60g Sainsbury's porridge oats, plus
1 tablespoon extra to decorate
125g dark brown soft sugar
2 teaspoons ground cinnamon
½ teaspoon bicarbonate of soda

2 medium eggs, beaten
150ml natural yogurt
1 teaspoon vanilla extract
90ml sunflower oil
180g raisins
3 tablespoons clear honey

1 Preheat the oven to 200°C, fan 180°C, gas 6. Place 10 paper cases (we've used Sainsbury's patterned muffin cases) in a 12-hole muffin tin.

2 In a large bowl, mix together the flour, oats, sugar, cinnamon and bicarbonate of soda. In another bowl, mix together the eggs, yogurt, vanilla extract and sunflower oil. Add the egg mixture to the flour mixture and stir well. Add the raisins and stir, but do not over-mix.

3 Spoon the mixture into the muffin cases and bake for 18-20 minutes.

4 Remove from the oven, trickle about 1 teaspoon honey over the top of each muffin, sprinkle with porridge oats and serve warm.

Per serving: 310 cals, 11.3g fat, 1.9g sat fat, 29.9g total sugars, 0.4g salt

Oaty banana mini muffins

Preheat the oven to 180°C, fan 160°C, gas 4. Line mini muffin tins with Sainsbury's petit four cases. Sift together 250g plain flour and 2 teaspoons baking powder, then stir in 75g porridge oats. In a separate bowl, beat together 3 eggs, 175g caster sugar, 250ml sunflower oil and a pinch of salt. Fold into the flour, along with 2 chopped bananas. Spoon into the petit four cases, sprinkle with oats and bake for 15 minutes, until golden.

MAKES 36   Prep time: 10 minutes   Cook time: 15 minutes

Each: 130 cals, 7.8g fat, 0.9g sat fat, 6.4g total sugars, trace salt

Makes 12
Prep time: 15 minutes,
plus cooling time
Cook time: 20 minutes

Classic cupcakes
with buttercream icing

These light, fluffy cupcakes with rainbow-coloured icing are simply irresistible

115g salted butter, softened
115g caster sugar
1 teaspoon vanilla essence
2 medium eggs
140g self-raising flour

FOR THE BUTTERCREAM ICING
150g unsalted butter, softened
250g icing sugar
a few drops of yellow, pink and green
food colouring
silver balls, pink glimmer sugar and
sprinkles, to decorate

1 Preheat the oven to 180°C, fan 160°C, gas 4. Line a 12-hole cupcake tin with cake cases – here we used Sainsbury's patterned cake cases.

2 Using an electric hand mixer, beat the butter and sugar together until light and fluffy. Add the vanilla essence, eggs and 1 tablespoon flour. Beat until combined, then add the remaining flour and whisk again.

3 Divide the mixture between the cake cases and bake for 20 minutes, until risen. Leave in the tin for a couple of minutes, then transfer the cakes to a wire rack and leave to cool completely.

4 Meanwhile, make the icing. Beat the butter in a large bowl, then add half the icing sugar and whisk until smooth. Add the remaining icing sugar and continue beating until creamy.

5 Divide the icing between 3 bowls and colour each differently for a pastel rainbow of cupcakes. A little food colouring goes a long way, so start with a drop or two and mix well.

6 Spoon the icing into a piping bag fitted with a large star nozzle. Hold the nozzle end with one hand (usually your writing hand). Squeeze the top of the bag with your other hand to make the icing flow through. Start by making a circle around the edge of the cakes and work towards the middle, making a spiral. Decorate with sprinkles before serving.

Per serving: 344 cals, 19.3g fat, 12.5g sat fat, 31.9g total sugars, 0.1g salt

Makes 8
Prep time: 25 minutes,
plus cooling time
Cook time: 25 minutes

Eclairs

Fabulously light choux pastry filled with cream and topped with chocolate

60g plain flour (preferably strong plain flour)
50g unsalted butter, cut into pieces
2 large eggs, beaten

FOR THE FILLING AND TOPPING
1 x 300ml pot Sainsbury's double cream
1 tablespoon icing sugar
100g dark chocolate
25g unsalted butter

1 Preheat the oven to 200°C, fan 180°C, gas 6.

2 Sieve the flour onto a small piece of baking parchment. Gently heat the butter in a small pan with 150ml cold water, until the butter has melted, then bring to the boil. Once the mixture reaches boiling point, remove immediately from the heat and tip in the flour all at once. Beat with a wooden spoon until the mixture forms a smooth ball, then leave to cool completely.

3 Using an electric hand mixer, beat the eggs into the mixture a little at a time, mixing thoroughly between each addition, until you get a smooth, glossy paste. Spoon into a piping bag fitted with a plain 1.5cm nozzle. Pipe 8 eclairs onto a non-stick baking sheet, leaving a gap between each one. Bake for 10 minutes, then increase the heat to 220°C, fan 200°C, gas 7 and bake for a further 15 minutes. Remove and cool on a wire rack. Using a sharp knife, make a small cut in the side of each eclair to allow the steam to escape.

4 To make the filling, whisk the cream until soft peaks are formed. Sift in the icing sugar and fold through. Spoon into a piping bag fitted with a 1cm nozzle and fill each eclair using the opening made earlier.

5 Melt the chocolate and butter together in a small bowl in the microwave or over a pan of simmering hot water. Leave to cool slightly, until it forms a thick, coating consistency, then spoon over the eclairs and leave to set.

Per serving: 361 cals, 31.6g fat, 19.5g sat fat, 8.4g total sugars, trace salt

Makes 12
Prep time: 20 minutes
Cook time: 25 minutes

Eccles cakes

These traditional cakes have a spiced fruit filling wrapped in rich flaky pastry

FOR THE FILLING

15g unsalted butter, softened
50g light brown soft sugar
½ teaspoon ground cinnamon
75g currants
25g mixed peel
¼ teaspoon freshly ground nutmeg
zest of ½ an orange

FOR THE PASTRY

1 x 500g pack Sainsbury's puff pastry
flour, for dusting
1 medium egg, beaten
1 tablespoon caster sugar

1   Preheat the oven to 180°C, fan 160°C, gas 4.

2   Mix all the ingredients for the filling together in a small bowl.

3   Roll out the puff pastry on a floured surface until about 0.3cm thick.
    Cut out 12 discs using a 10cm round cutter.

4   Place 1 heaped teaspoon of the filling into the centre of each disc. Brush
    the edge with a little beaten egg and draw the edges together to make
    a purse, squeezing tightly to seal them.

5   Using the palm of your hand, flatten the cakes to become discs, making
    sure they are thin enough to see the currants underneath. Brush each
    cake with more beaten egg, then sprinkle with caster sugar. Using a sharp
    knife, make 3 parallel cuts on top.

6   Bake for 20-25 minutes, or until the pastry is golden brown.

Per serving: 237 cals, 12.6g fat, 7.7g sat fat, 12.2g total sugars, 0.2g salt

Makes 20
Prep time: 15 minutes,
plus cooling time
Cook time: 35 minutes

Chocolate & cherry cheesecake brownies

Chocolate and cherries make a winning combination, especially in these scrumptious cheesecake brownies

150g unsalted butter, softened, plus extra for greasing
1 x 200g bar Sainsbury's Belgian plain chocolate, roughly chopped
275g Sainsbury's Fairtrade caster sugar

5 medium eggs
75g plain flour, sifted
1 x 300g pack Sainsbury's soft cheese
200g Sainsbury's frozen dark sweet cherries, thawed

1 Preheat the oven to 180°C, fan 160°C, gas 4. Grease a 20 x 30cm baking tin and line with baking parchment.

2 Combine the butter and chocolate in a bowl set over a saucepan of simmering water and stir continuously until melted, making sure the bowl doesn't touch the water. Cool, then stir in 225g caster sugar. Beat in 3 eggs, one by one, then mix in the flour and set aside.

3 In a separate bowl, whisk the soft cheese with the remaining 50g caster sugar and 2 eggs, until creamy. Drop alternate spoonfuls of each mixture into the prepared baking tin. Using a spoon, swirl together to create a marbled effect.

4 Scatter the cherries on top and bake for 30-35 minutes. Place on a wire rack, cover with foil and allow to cool before serving.

Per serving: 243 cals, 14.6g fat, 8.9g sat fat, 20.8g total sugars, 0.1g salt

Seasonal tip:
When cherries are in season, you can make these brownies with 200g fresh cherries, stoned

'A heavenly combination of cheesecake and brownie'

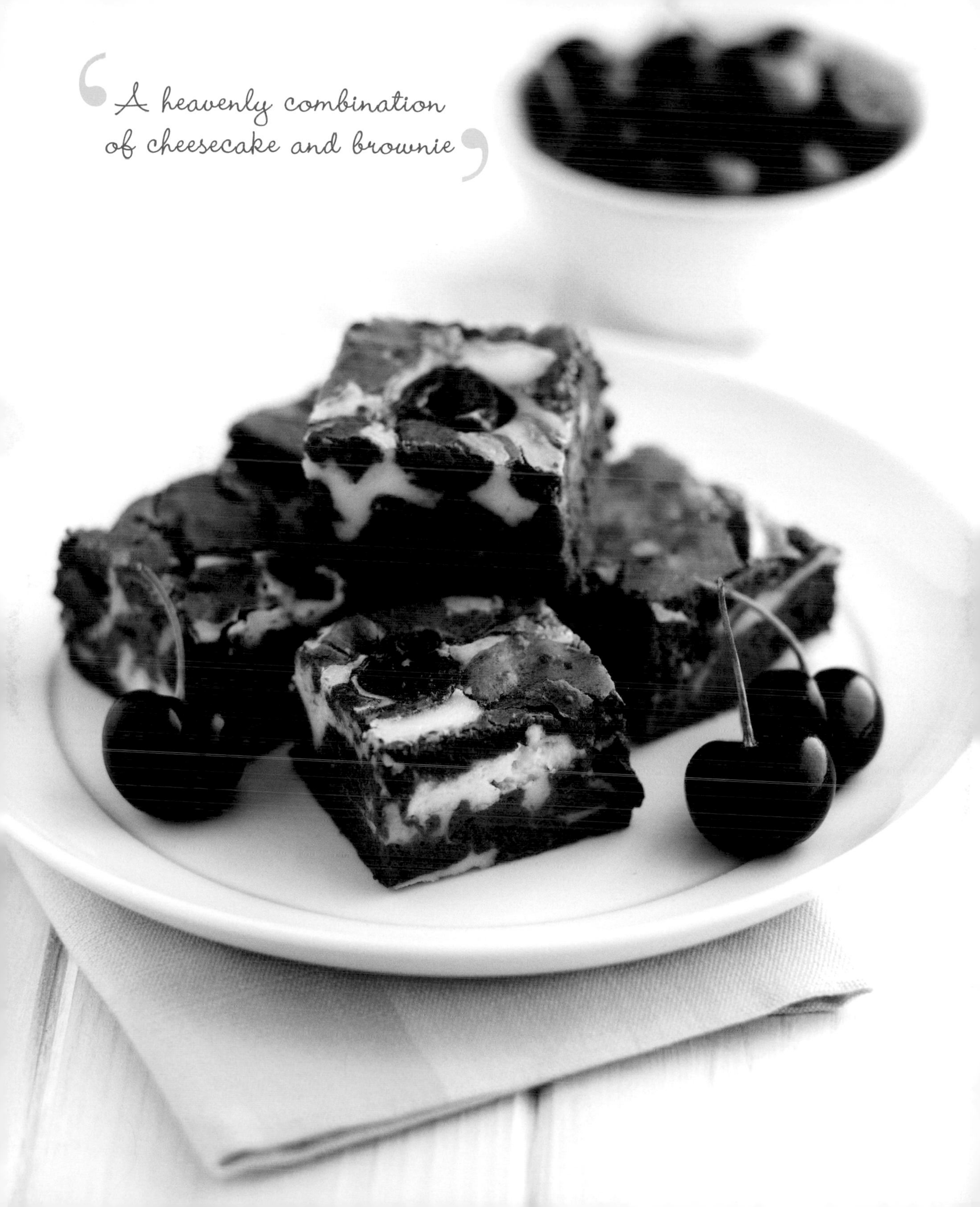

Makes 30
Prep time: 15 minutes,
plus overnight chilling
Cook time: 20 minutes

Macadamia nut blondies

With their irresistible chewy texture and the rich flavour of brown sugar instead of chocolate, blondies are a fantastic alternative to brownies

125g unsalted butter, softened
400g Sainsbury's Fairtrade light brown soft sugar
2 medium eggs
2 tablespoons vanilla extract
125g plain flour

2 teaspoons baking powder
½ teaspoon salt
80g macadamia nuts, roughly chopped
50g desiccated coconut
100g white chocolate, roughly chopped

1 Preheat the oven to 180°C, fan 160°C, gas 4. Line a 36 x 24cm baking tray with baking parchment, allowing it to extend up the sides of the tray to form a 5cm collar.

2 Using an electric hand mixer, whisk together the butter and sugar. Add the eggs, whisking in one at a time, and the vanilla extract. Add the flour, baking powder and salt, and mix to combine. Stir in the nuts, coconut and chocolate.

3 Spread the mixture out in the tray as evenly as possible. Bake for 10 minutes, then rotate 180 degrees and continue to bake for another 10 minutes. Be careful not to over-bake.

4 Leave in the tray to cool completely, then chill in the fridge overnight. Once completely cold, cut into bars or squares to serve. They will have a lovely crunchy, slightly chewy texture.

Per serving: 155 cals, 8.1g fat, 4.4g sat fat, 15.4g total sugars, 0.2g salt

These tempting little squares are full of nuts and white chocolate

Makes 18
Prep time: 15 minutes,
plus chilling time
Cook time: 15 minutes

Pink grapefruit tarts

These tantalisingly tangy treats are perfect for afternoon tea

175g plain flour, plus extra for dusting
100g butter, cold from the fridge, cubed
2 tablespoons caster sugar

1 egg yolk
about 200g pink grapefruit curd (see below)
icing sugar, for dusting

1 Sift the flour into a bowl. Rub in the butter until it resembles breadcrumbs, then stir in the sugar. Make a well in the mixture and add the egg yolk and 1 tablespoon cold water. Use a round-bladed knife to bring everything together, adding a drop more water if necessary. Use your hands to form a dough, handling as little as possible. (Alternatively, make the dough in a food processor to save time.) Wrap the dough in clingfilm and chill for 20 minutes.

2 Preheat the oven to 200°C, fan 180°C, gas 6. Roll out the pastry on a lightly floured surface. Stamp out rounds with a 7cm fluted cutter and gently press into cupcake tins. Prick the bases with a fork and chill for 15 minutes.

3 Bake the tarts for 10 minutes, until crisp and light golden brown. Spoon about 2 teaspoons grapefruit curd into each tart and bake for another 3–5 minutes, until the curd is just beginning to bubble at the edges. Leave to cool, then dust with icing sugar.

Per serving: 128 cals, 7.4g fat, 4.7g sat fat, 5.7g total sugars, trace salt

Pink grapefruit curd

Whisk 4 large eggs in a large, heavy-based pan, then whisk in the zest and juice of 2 pink grapefruit, the juice of 1 lemon, 350g golden caster sugar, 225g butter and 2 tablespoons cornflour. Warm gently over a very low heat, stirring constantly, for at least 30 minutes, until it's thick enough to coat the back of a spoon. Don't allow to boil. Strain through a sieve into clean, sterilised jars and allow to cool completely. Store in the fridge for up to 1 month.

MAKES 750G Prep time: 10 minutes Cook time: 30 minutes

Per 100g: 373 cals, 21.9g fat, 13g sat fat, 35.4g total sugars, 0.1g salt

“These delightfully zesty tarts are made with homemade pink grapefruit curd”

Makes 8
Prep time: 15 minutes
Cook time: 15 minutes

Blueberry buttermilk scones

These fruity scones are great with our easy-to-make, freezable blackberry jam

225g self-raising flour, plus extra for dusting
75g unsalted butter, at room temperature,
plus extra for greasing
50g caster sugar
1 x 75g pack Sainsbury's dried blueberries
1 large egg, beaten

3-4 tablespoons buttermilk

TO SERVE
½ x 227ml pack Taste the Difference
Cornish clotted cream
blackberry freezer jam (see below)

1   Preheat the oven to 190°C, fan 170°C, gas 5. Sift the flour and a pinch of salt into a mixing bowl. Rub in the butter until it resembles breadcrumbs.

2   Stir in the sugar and blueberries. Add the egg and 3 tablespoons buttermilk, and mix with a palette knife. Only add another tablespoon of buttermilk if the mixture seems very dry. Using your hands, form it into a soft dough.

3   On a floured surface, gently roll out the dough until about 2.5cm thick. Cut out 8 rounds using a floured 6cm cutter and place on a lightly greased baking tray. Bake for 10-15 minutes, until golden. Serve with the cream and jam.

Per serving: 247 cals, 9.1g fat, 5.5g sat fat, 13.7g total sugars, 0.3g salt

Blackberry freezer jam

Place 600g blackberries in a large mixing bowl and crush with a potato masher. Fold in 1kg caster sugar, then add 1 x 250g bottle Certo liquid pectin (in the baking aisle) and 2 tablespoons lemon juice. Stir thoroughly. Pour into sterilised storage containers or jars, put on the lids and stand at room temperature for 24 hours. This soft-set jam will freeze for up to 1 year. Remove from the freezer at least 1 hour before you want to use it, and store in the fridge for up to 3 weeks.

MAKES 2 LITRES   Prep time: 10 minutes, plus standing time

Per 100g: 238 cals, trace fat, trace sat fat, 58.1g total sugars, trace salt

*Served warm with jam
and fresh clotted cream,
these won't last long*

Makes 6
Prep time: 40 minutes,
plus chilling time
Cook time: 20 minutes

Banoffee tarts

An irresistible combination of banana, caramel and cream, banoffee tarts have become a modern classic

180g plain flour
120g butter, cold from the fridge, cubed
3 tablespoons caster sugar
1 egg yolk, mixed with 1 tablespoon cold water
75g dark chocolate, melted

½ x 397g tin Carnation caramel
2 small bananas, sliced
200ml double cream
¼ teaspoon ground cinnamon
2 teaspoons cocoa powder

1 Sift the flour into a large bowl. Lightly rub in the butter with your fingertips, until the mixture resembles breadcrumbs. Stir in the sugar, then the egg yolk and water mixture, and use a round-bladed knife to bring everything together. Use your hands to form a dough, handling it as little as possible. (Alternatively, make the dough in a food processor to save time.) Wrap the dough in clingfilm, then chill in the fridge for 20 minutes.

2 Preheat the oven to 200°C, fan 180°C fan, gas 6. Roll out the pastry to a thickness of 0.5cm, then cut into 6 pieces. Line 6 individual 10.5cm tart tins with the pastry and chill again for 20 minutes.

3 Line the pastry cases with baking parchment and fill with baking beans or uncooked rice. Bake 'blind' for 15 minutes, then remove the paper and beans and bake for a further 2 minutes, or until golden.

4 Pour or brush the melted chocolate around the inside of the tart cases and allow it to harden for 5 minutes in the fridge. Pour the caramel into the pastry cases and top with the banana slices.

5 Whisk the double cream until it forms stiff peaks, then spoon on top of the tarts. Dust with the cinnamon and cocoa powder and serve.

Per serving: 654 cals, 39.8g fat, 25.4g sat fat, 41.6g total sugars, 0.1g salt

Makes 12
Prep time: 10 minutes,
pus cooling time
Cook time: 20 minutes

Jammy fairy cakes

Little ones will enjoy getting their hands sticky if there's a fairy cake reward

115g unsalted butter, softened
115g caster sugar
1 teaspoon vanilla essence
2 medium free-range eggs

140g self-raising flour
12 teaspoons strawberry jam
icing sugar, for dusting

1 Preheat the oven to 180ºC, fan 160ºC, gas 4 and line a 12-hole cupcake tin with paper cases.

2 Whisk the butter and sugar together until light and fluffy, then add the vanilla essence, eggs and 1 tablespoon flour. Whisk until combined, then add the remaining flour and whisk again.

3 Pour half the mixture into the cases. Add 1 teaspoon jam to each case and top with the remaining mixture. Bake for 20 minutes, until risen. Leave in the tin for 2 minutes, then cool on a wire rack. Dust with icing sugar before serving.

Per serving: 180 cals, 9g fat, 5.6g sat fat, 13.7g total sugars, 0.1g salt

Mini orange & lemon muffins

Preheat the oven to 180ºC, fan 160ºC, gas 4. Place the finely chopped segments of 1 orange, and any juice, in a large bowl. Add the zest of 1 lemon, 100g caster sugar, 1 egg, beaten, 100ml buttermilk, 50g melted unsalted butter, ½ teaspoon baking powder and 200g self-raising flour, sifted. Mix well. Spoon into greased and floured mini muffin tins and bake for 15-20 minutes, until golden. Mix icing sugar with orange or lemon juice, and drizzle over.

MAKES 36   Prep time: 15 minutes   Cook time: 20 minutes

Each: 64 cals, 1.4g fat, 0.9g sat fat, 7.9g total sugars, trace salt

Makes 12
Prep time: 30 minutes,
plus cooling time
Cook time: 20 minutes

Butterfly cakes

The kids will love helping you make these cute-as-a-button fairy cakes

60g unsalted butter, softened
125g Sainsbury's Fairtrade caster sugar
1 Sainsbury's free-range Woodland
medium egg
130g self-raising flour, sifted
60g ground almonds
100ml semi-skimmed milk

FOR THE BUTTERCREAM ICING
100g icing sugar, sifted
75g unsalted butter, softened
1 tablespoon semi-skimmed milk
50g white chocolate, melted
20g Sainsbury's princess sprinkles

1 Preheat the oven to 180°C, fan 160°C, gas 4. Line a 12-hole cupcake tin
with cases (here we've used Sainsbury's patterned cake cases).

2 In a large bowl, beat the butter with the sugar until light and fluffy. Whisk
in the egg. In a separate bowl, mix together the flour and ground almonds.

3 Alternately mix the flour mixture and the milk into the butter, egg and
sugar mixture. Spoon into the cake cases. Bake for 20 minutes, or until a
skewer inserted into them comes out clean. Leave to cool on a wire rack.

4 Meanwhile, make the icing. In a bowl, gradually mix the icing sugar into
the butter, then beat until light and creamy. Add the milk and melted
chocolate and whisk well into the buttercream.

5 Once the cakes are cool, cut out a round of sponge from the top, then
cut that in half. Brush a little buttercream icing onto the top side of the
2 halves and dip in the sprinkles. Place a teaspoon of buttercream into
the cakes, then place the sponge halves on top to create butterfly wings.

Per serving: 272 cals, 14.2g fat, 7.3g sat fat, 24.5g total sugars, 0.1g salt

Time-saving tip:
Try using Sainsbury's fairy cake mix to make these
butterfly cakes

puddings, tarts & desserts

Serves 6
Prep time: 10 minutes, plus standing time
Cook time: 1 hour

Strawberry & cream bread & butter pudding

Double cream and strawberry jam give this classic pud a tasty twist

6 thick slices day-old white bread, crusts removed
50g unsalted butter, softened, plus extra for greasing
3 tablespoons reduced-sugar strawberry jam
3 large eggs

1 x 300ml pot Sainsbury's double cream
200ml semi-skimmed milk
2 tablespoons caster sugar
seeds of 1 vanilla pod
½ tablespoon demerara sugar
15g flaked almonds

1 Spread each slice of bread with butter, then spread 3 of the buttered slices with the jam.

2 Top each jam slice with a buttered slice, butter facing upwards, then cut each 'sandwich' into 4 triangles. Arrange in a buttered 1.5-litre ovenproof dish, pointing upwards.

3 Beat together the eggs, cream, milk, caster sugar and vanilla seeds, then pour over the bread. Leave to stand for 15 minutes to allow the custard to soak in. Meanwhile, preheat the oven to 160°C, fan 140°C, gas 3.

4 Sprinkle on the demerara sugar and almonds and bake for 50–60 minutes, until the custard is set. Serve immediately. Great with custard or cream.

Per serving: 484 cals, 37g fat, 20.9g sat fat, 15.7g total sugars, 0.4g salt

'This creamy bread and butter pudding is wonderfully comforting'

Serves 4
Prep time: 15 minutes
Cook time: 30 minutes

Individual strawberry & raspberry puddings

Ginger adds a warming kick to these berry-packed puds

½ x 400g pack Sainsbury's strawberries, hulled and halved
½ x 250g pack Sainsbury's raspberries
1 ball of stem ginger, finely chopped, plus 2 tablespoons syrup from the jar

90g unsalted butter, softened
100g caster sugar
100g self-raising flour, sifted
2 large eggs, beaten
2 tablespoons semi-skimmed milk

1 Preheat the oven to 190°C, fan 170°C, gas 5.

2 Arrange the berries in 4 ramekins. Scatter over the ginger and syrup.

3 Whisk together the butter and sugar until pale and creamy. Gradually whisk in the flour and eggs alternately, adding the milk to loosen the mixture.

4 Spoon the batter over the berries and place the ramekins on a baking tray. Bake for 30 minutes.

Per serving: 454 cals, 22.7g fat, 12.5g sat fat, 35.4g total sugars, 0.3g salt

Blackberry & apple crumble

Preheat the oven to 190°C, fan 170°C, gas 5. In a bowl, rub together 115g butter and 200g plain flour. Stir in 120g light muscovado sugar and 1 teaspoon ground cinnamon. In a 1.5-litre ovenproof dish, mix together 300g blackberries, 2 Bramley cooking apples, peeled, cored and cut into small pieces, and 50g caster sugar. Drizzle with the juice of 1 lemon. Sprinkle over the crumble topping and pat down with your hand. Bake for 30–35 minutes, until golden brown.

SERVES 4   Prep time: 20 minutes   Cook time: 35 minutes

Each: 635 cals, 24.5g fat, 14.5g sat fat, 55.2g total sugars, trace salt

'These easy-to-make, individual puds are full of juicy summer berries'

Pecan pie

This deliciously rich pie, topped with syrupy pecans, is an American classic

Serves 10
Prep time: 20 minutes,
plus chilling time
Cook time: 1 hour,
5 minutes

200g plain flour
125g unsalted butter
2 tablespoons icing sugar
4 medium eggs
225g light brown soft sugar
170g golden syrup, plus 1 tablespoon to glaze

½ teaspoon salt
50g unsalted butter, melted
2 tablespoons flour
350g pecan halves, 200g chopped and
the rest left whole

1   In a bowl, rub together the flour and butter until it resembles fine breadcrumbs. Stir in the icing sugar. Add enough water to mix into a firm dough. Roll out and use to line a 24cm loose-based tart tin. Chill in the fridge for 20 minutes.

2   Preheat the oven to 200°C, fan 180°C, gas 6.

3   Line the tart case with baking parchment, then fill with baking beans or uncooked rice and bake 'blind' for 10 minutes. Remove the baking beans and bake for a further 5 minutes, until firm.

4   To make the filling, whisk the eggs with the sugar in a bowl until combined. Add the golden syrup, salt and butter. Sieve in the flour and stir. Add the chopped pecans and pour the mixture into the pastry case. Arrange the whole pecans on top.

5   Bake for 10 minutes, then reduce the heat to 160°C, fan 140°C, gas 3 and bake for 30-40 minutes, until the centre no longer feels wobbly.

6   Gently heat 1 tablespoon golden syrup and brush over the top of the pie to glaze. Leave to cool before slicing.

Per serving: 651 cals, 41.7g fat, 12.8g sat fat, 41.9g total sugars, 0.5g salt

Time-saving tip
Try using a ready-made sweet pastry case instead of making your own pastry

'This wonderful pie has a fabulous syrupy flavour and chewy texture'

Serves 6
Prep time: 15 minutes
Cook time: 25 minutes

Individual chocolate soufflés

These chocolate delights are light, fluffy and easy to make

50g unsalted butter, plus an extra 30g, melted, for greasing the ramekins
3 tablespoons caster sugar, plus extra for lining the ramekins
2 tablespoons plain flour

250ml semi-skimmed milk
130g Sainsbury's Belgian dark cooking chocolate, roughly chopped
4 medium eggs, separated
icing sugar, for dusting

---

1 Preheat the oven to 200°C, fan 180°C, gas 6. Using a pastry brush, lightly brush the insides of 6 ramekins with the melted butter, using upward strokes. Coat with a little caster sugar, then place on a baking tray.

2 Melt 50g butter in a small saucepan over a medium heat. Add the flour and stir with a wooden spoon, until smooth and starting to bubble. Gradually pour the milk into the pan and continue stirring until the mixture is thick and smooth. Allow the sauce to simmer on a low heat for about 2 minutes, then remove from the heat.

3 Tip in the chocolate and remaining 3 tablespoons caster sugar, and mix until melted and combined. Add the egg yolks, one at a time, beating well between each addition. Transfer to a medium bowl.

4 Using an electric hand mixer, whisk the egg whites in a bowl until soft peaks are formed. Tip half the egg whites over the chocolate mixture. Using a metal spoon, lift and fold the whites through the mixture. Add the remaining egg whites and fold through - your mixture should look spongy and frothy.

5 Spoon into the ramekins to just below the rim. Pop the tray in the oven and bake for 15 minutes. Resist opening the oven or they'll sink - they'll be ready when the centre is well risen. When pressed, they should yield but not feel liquid-like. Dust with icing sugar and serve immediately.

Per serving: 337 cals, 21.1g fat, 11.5g sat fat, 23.9g total sugars, 0.2g salt

Rhubarb & orange custard tart

Serves 8
Prep time: 25 minutes, plus chilling time
Cook time: 1 hour, 20 minutes

This delicious dessert has the satisfyingly smooth texture of a custard tart, with added tang and zest coming from the rhubarb and orange

1 x 375g pack Sainsbury's dessert pastry
flour, for dusting
400g rhubarb
80g granulated sugar
30g unsalted butter, at room temperature
3 tablespoons caster sugar

3 tablespoons ground almonds
zest of 1 small orange
2 large eggs
75ml double cream
icing sugar, to dust

1 Roll out the pastry on a floured surface and use to line a 24cm loose-based tart tin. Cover with clingfilm and chill in the fridge for 20 minutes. Preheat the oven to 160°C, fan 140°C, gas 3.

2 Wash and trim the rhubarb and cut into 3cm lengths. Place in an ovenproof dish, sprinkle with the granulated sugar and cover with foil. Bake for 15-20 minutes, until just tender but still holding its shape. Leave to cool completely. When the rhubarb is cold, strain it, reserving the juice.

3 Increase the oven temperature to 200°C, fan 180°C, gas 6. Line the pastry case with baking parchment and fill with baking beans or uncooked rice. Bake 'blind' for 18-20 minutes, removing the beans and baking parchment for the last 5 minutes. Set aside and reduce the oven temperature to 180°C, fan 160°C, gas 4.

4 Meanwhile, cream the butter with the caster sugar in a bowl using an electric hand mixer. Add the almonds and orange zest, then the eggs, one at a time. Add the double cream and 100ml reserved rhubarb juice, and stir in gently.

5 Spoon the baked rhubarb over the pastry base and carefully pour over the cream mixture. Bake for 35-40 minutes, until set and lightly browned. Allow to cool - this tart is best eaten at room temperature - then dust with icing sugar. Great served with lightly whipped cream.

Per serving: 440 cals, 27.1g fat, 12g sat fat, 23.4g total sugars, 0.3g salt

‘Put a spin on a traditional custard tart with tangy rhubarb’

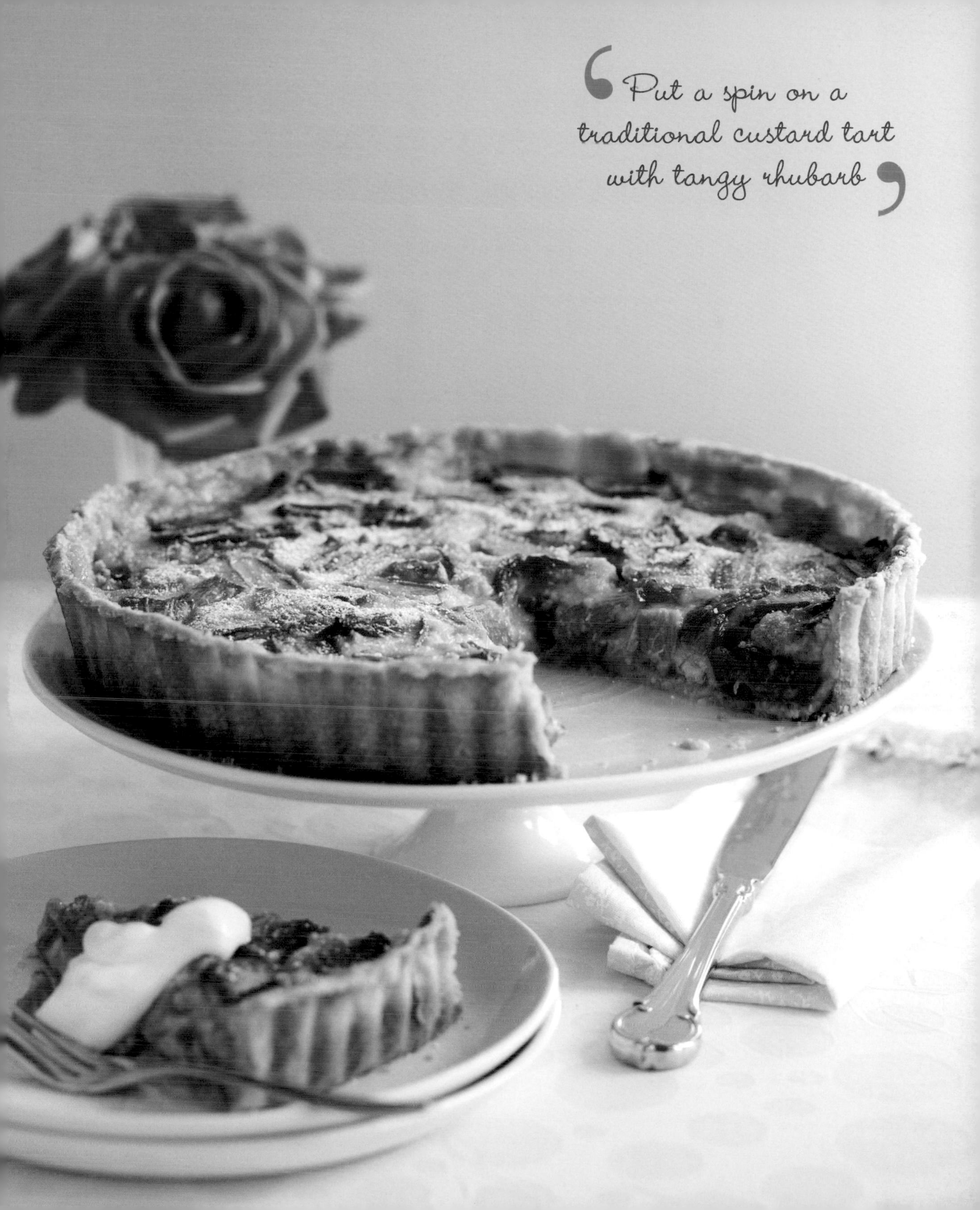

Serves 6
Prep time: 10 minutes,
plus chilling and
cooling time
Cook time: 40 minutes

Apple tarte tatin

A classic French recipe using gorgeous British apples

½ x 500g pack Taste the Difference puff pastry
flour, for dusting
5 Braeburn apples, peeled, cored and
quartered

165g granulated sugar
2 teaspoons lemon juice
½ teaspoon vanilla extract
50g unsalted butter

---

1 Preheat the oven to 200°C, fan 180°C, gas 6. Roll out the puff pastry on a lightly floured surface and cut out a 28cm circle. Place in the fridge to chill for 15 minutes.

2 In a bowl, toss the apple quarters with 55g sugar, the lemon juice and the vanilla extract. Set aside.

3 In a 24cm ovenproof frying pan, melt the butter over a medium heat and add the remaining 110g sugar. Turn down to a gentle heat and leave, without stirring, for 4–5 minutes, until the mixture turns a golden caramel colour – don't worry if it looks as if it has separated, as this is normal. Remove from the heat.

4 Arrange the apples on top of the caramel, rounded side down, in a circular pattern. Cover with the pastry circle, tucking the edges inside the pan around the apples. Bake in the oven for 35 minutes, until puffed and golden.

5 Remove from the oven and allow to cool for 10 minutes. Invert a plate over the pan and turn over. Serve warm.

Per serving: 395 cals, 18g fat, 11.6g sat fat, 37.7g total sugars, 0.1g salt

‘The caramelised
apples in this tarte tatin
are gorgeously gooey’

Serves 8
Prep time: 20 minutes, plus cooling time
Cook time: 25 minutes

Quick raspberry tart

This tart is amazingly easy. You can use low-fat cream cheese instead of quark

375g ready-rolled puff pastry
flour, for dusting
3 tablespoons apple or orange juice
500g raspberries
100g unsalted butter, at room temperature

100g icing sugar, sifted
1 x 250g tub be good to yourself quark
100ml half-fat crème fraîche
zest of 1 lemon and juice of ½ a lemon
½ x 1 egg, beaten

1 Preheat the oven to 220°C, fan 200°C, gas 7.

2 Unroll the pastry on a floured baking tray. Prick with a fork. Cover with another floured baking tray to weigh it down. Bake for 15-20 minutes until almost cooked.

3 Pour the juice over the raspberries in a bowl and leave for 10 minutes. Cream the butter and icing sugar together in a large bowl. Beat in the quark, crème fraîche, lemon juice and half the zest. In another bowl, mash one-third of the raspberries and their juice with a fork, then mix into the whole raspberries.

4 Remove the top baking tray from the pastry. Brush the pastry with the egg and bake for a further 4-5 minutes, until golden. Cool completely, then spread with the quark mixture and top with the berries. Sprinkle with the remaining lemon zest and serve at once.

Per serving: 462 cals, 29.6g fat, 15.1g sat fat, 19.6g total sugars, 0.8g salt

Apricot & almond tart

Preheat the oven to 220°C, fan 200°C, gas 7. Unroll 375g ready-rolled puff pastry and cut into 6 rectangles. Place on a non-stick baking tray. Sprinkle with 1 tablespoon ground almonds, then arrange 9 stoned and quartered apricots on top. Sprinkle each rectangle with 60g demerara sugar and 1 tablespoon amaretto, then bake for 15-20 minutes, until the pastry is golden and cooked. Dust with icing sugar and serve. Great with crème fraîche.

SERVES 6   Prep time: 10 minutes   Cook time: 20 minutes

Each: 329 cals, 18g fat, 11g sat fat, 15.6g total sugars, 0.2g salt

'This raspberry tart looks impressive but is really easy to make'

Serves 8
Prep time: 20 minutes,
plus chilling time
Cook time: 30 minutes

Strawberry tart

Plump, glazed strawberries and buttery pastry create a timeless classic

175g plain flour, plus extra for dusting
100g butter, cold from the fridge, cubed
70g caster sugar
1 egg yolk
100ml double cream

200g mascarpone
seeds of 1 vanilla pod
1 x 400g pack Sainsbury's strawberries, hulled
and halved, with 1 left whole to decorate
2 tablespoons apricot jam, melted

1 To make the pastry, sift the flour into a bowl. Lightly rub in the butter with your fingertips, until the mixture resembles breadcrumbs. Stir in 30g sugar. Make a well in the mixture and add the egg yolk and 1 tablespoon cold water. Use a round-bladed knife to bring everything together, adding a drop more water if necessary. Use your hands to form a dough, handling it as little as possible. (Alternatively, you could make the pastry in a food processor.) Wrap in clingfilm and chill in the fridge for 20 minutes. Preheat the oven to 190°C, fan 170°C, gas 5.

2 Roll out the pastry on a lightly floured surface and line a 19cm loose-based sandwich tin or a 20cm loose-based fluted tart tin. Leave the pastry standing slightly higher than the top of the tin. Chill for 20 minutes.

3 Using a sharp knife, trim the top of the pastry case. Using the handle of a teaspoon, make indentations along the edge. Line the pastry with baking parchment, then fill with baking beans or uncooked rice and bake 'blind' for 15 minutes. Remove the beans and baking parchment and bake for a further 10-12 minutes, until crisp and golden brown. Leave to cool.

4 Using a food processor, whisk together the cream, mascarpone, vanilla seeds and remaining 40g sugar. Spread the mascarpone mixture over the pastry case and cover with the strawberries. Place 1 whole strawberry in the centre and brush the lot with the melted apricot jam. Serve on the day of making.

Per serving: 400 cals, 27.7g fat, 17.8g sat fat, 16.2g total sugars, trace salt

Time-saving tip
Use a Sainsbury's sweet pastry case instead. Brush the insides and edges with 1 tablespoon double cream, bake for 10 minutes, then follow the recipe

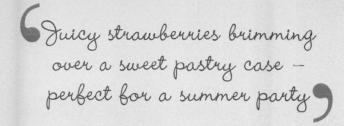

Serves 12
Prep time: 25 minutes,
plus chilling time
Cook time: 30 minutes

Salted caramel tart

Never tried salt and chocolate before? This recipe will leave you hooked...

170g unsalted butter
50g golden caster sugar
2 medium egg yolks
275g plain flour, plus extra for dusting
25g Sainsbury's Fairtrade cocoa powder
300g Carnation caramel
200ml double cream

2 x 100g bars Taste the Difference dark
Belgian cooking chocolate, roughly chopped
200g light muscovado sugar
1 ½ teaspoons Maldon sea salt
1 x 100g pack Taste the Difference cocoa
dusted almonds

1 In a food processor, pulse the butter, caster sugar, egg yolks, flour and cocoa powder until it comes together. Wrap in clingfilm and chill in the fridge for 1 hour.

2 On a surface dusted with flour, roll out the pastry and use to line a 24cm loose-based tart tin. Trim the excess. Chill for 20 minutes to help prevent it shrinking during cooking.

3 Preheat the oven to 180ºC, fan 160ºC, gas 4. Line the pastry with baking parchment, fill with baking beans or uncooked rice and bake 'blind' for 20 minutes. Remove the parchment and beans and cook for a further 5 minutes, or until the base is dry. Leave to cool slightly, then spread with the caramel.

4 Place the cream, chocolate, muscovado sugar and sea salt in a bowl over a pan of lightly simmering water until melted, thick and glossy. Pour into the tart case, scatter over the almonds and chill for 2 hours, until set.

Per serving: 489 cals, 31.1g fat, 19.3g sat fat, 46.2g total sugars, 0.7g salt

Tip
If you prefer, you could replace the cocoa-dusted almonds with whole almonds, pecans or hazelnuts

"The sweetness of the chocolate works fabulously with the tingle of salt"

Serves 8
Prep time: 30 minutes,
plus cooling time
Cook time: 50 minutes

Baked raspberry cheesecake

Swirls of raspberry jam give this baked cheesecake a professional look

1 x 200g pack Sainsbury's ginger snaps, crushed
50g unsalted butter, melted, plus extra for greasing
500g full fat cream cheese, softened
75g caster sugar

1 teaspoon vanilla extract
2 large eggs
85g Taste the Difference raspberry conserve, warmed through
50g fresh raspberries

1 Preheat the oven to 150°C, fan 130°C, gas 2. Lightly grease an 18cm round springform tin and line with baking parchment.

2 Whizz the ginger snaps to a fine dust in a food processor, then mix with the melted butter. Press into the bottom of the lined tin. Bake for 10 minutes, then remove from the oven and allow to cool slightly.

3 For the filling, use an electric hand mixer to beat together the cream cheese, sugar, vanilla and eggs. Pour into the tin and gently spoon over the warmed raspberry conserve, creating swirls that stay suspended on top of the mixture.

4 Bake for 35-40 minutes, or until the filling has set. Remove from the oven and allow to cool in the tin. Once cool, transfer to a serving plate and decorate with the raspberries.

Per serving: 398 cals, 24.5g fat, 14.5g sat fat, 26.3g total sugars, 0.7g salt

Serves 8
Prep time: 20 minutes,
plus chilling time
Cook time: 55 minutes

Plum & almond frangipane tart

A rich almond filling gives this fruit tart a sophisticated, grown-up twist

235g plain flour
110g unsalted butter, cold from the fridge, cubed, plus 100g unsalted butter at room temperature
zest of 1 orange
100g caster sugar

2 medium eggs
½ x 200g pack Sainsbury's ground almonds
½ teaspoon Taste the Difference French almond extract
4 red plums, stoned and cut into wedges
3 teaspoons apricot jam, melted, to glaze

1 Sift 225g flour into a large bowl, along with a small pinch of salt. Lightly rub in the cubed butter with your fingertips, until the mixture resembles breadcrumbs. Stir in the orange zest. Sprinkle on 1½ tablespoons cold water and use a round-bladed knife to bring everything together. Gradually add another 1½ tablespoons water, and use your hands to form a dough, handling it as little as possible. Wrap in clingfilm and chill in the fridge for 20 minutes.

2 Roll out the pastry and use to line a 24cm loose-based tart tin. Chill in the fridge for 30 minutes.

3 Preheat the oven to 200°C, fan 180°C, gas 6. Line the pastry case with baking parchment, fill with baking beans or uncooked rice and bake 'blind' for 10-15 minutes, until the base is firm and dry. Remove from the oven and remove the beans and parchment. Reduce the oven to 180°C, fan 160°C, gas 4.

4 To make the filling, whisk together the room-temperature butter and sugar until pale. Add the eggs, one at a time, then fold in the almonds, almond extract and the remaining 10g flour. Whisk briskly for 1 minute, then set aside.

5 Spoon the filling into the pastry case, then scatter over the plums and press down gently. Bake on the middle shelf for 30-40 minutes, or until golden. Leave to cool in the tin, then brush with the apricot jam. Great with cream.

Per serving: 473 cals, 30.4g fat, 15.1g sat fat, 17.8g total sugars, trace salt

The sweet almond filling works perfectly with the baked plums

Serves 4
Prep time: 15 minutes
Cook time: 40 minutes

Apple pie

This is a foolproof recipe for the perfect, traditional apple pie

250g self-raising flour
50g icing sugar, sifted
125g unsalted butter, cubed
1 large egg, beaten, plus extra for glazing
a splash of milk

4 Bramley apples, peeled, cored and chopped
1 tablespoon cornflour
zest and juice of 1 lemon
50g granulated sugar
½ teaspoon each ground cinnamon and ginger

1 Pulse the flour, icing sugar and butter in a food processor until it resembles breadcrumbs. Add the egg and pulse until the dough comes together in a smooth ball, adding the milk if necessary. Wrap in clingfilm and chill in the fridge.

2 Meanwhile, in a bowl, mix together the apples, cornflour, lemon zest and juice, sugar and spices. Place in a 1-litre ovenproof dish and brush the edges with a little beaten egg. Preheat the oven to 190ºC, fan 170ºC, gas 5.

3 Roll out the pastry to a thickness of 0.5cm. Place over the apple mixture and pinch the edges to secure onto the rim. Make a 1cm hole in the centre and decorate the top with leaves made from leftover pastry, securing with beaten egg. Brush with beaten egg and bake for 20 minutes. Reduce the oven to 180ºC, fan 160ºC, gas 4 and cook for a further 15–20 minutes, until golden.

Per serving: 678 cals, 30.1g fat, 18.6g sat fat, 39.8g total sugars, 0.6g salt

Super-easy cherry lattice pie

This simple pie uses mostly frozen ingredients. Defrost 1 x 450g pack frozen Jus-rol shortcrust pastry sheets. Preheat the oven to 200ºC, fan 180ºC, gas 6. Use 1 pastry sheet to line a 1-litre pie dish, and brush the rim with water. Mix 1 x 480g pack Sainsbury's frozen cherries with 60g ground almonds and 3 tablespoons caster sugar, and tip in the dish. Slice lengths from another pastry sheet and weave over the pie. Press down the edges to seal and bake for 50 minutes.

SERVES 6 Prep time: 20 minutes Cook time: 50 minutes

Per slice: 520 cals, 29.7g fat, 13.8g sat fat, 19.7g total sugars, 0.8g salt

Makes 4
Prep time: 20 minutes
Cook time: 20 minutes

Melt-in-the-middle chocolate puds

Break open these fondant puddings to reveal a melting chocolate centre

150g unsalted butter
2-3 tablespoons Sainsbury's Fairtrade cocoa powder
200g dark chocolate, broken up

2 medium eggs, plus 2 extra yolks
100g caster sugar
25g plain flour
icing sugar, for dusting

1 Melt 25g butter in a saucepan. Using a pastry brush, coat 4 x 8.5cm diameter metal pudding moulds with the butter. Sprinkle with the cocoa powder, tapping out any excess. Preheat the oven to 180ºC, fan 160ºC, gas 4.

2 Place the chocolate and the remaining 125g butter in a bowl over a pan of gently simmering water. Heat gently until melted and smooth. Remove from the heat and cool for about 5 minutes.

3 Place the eggs, egg yolks and sugar into a bowl and whisk until the mixture is thick and pale and leaves a trail when the whisk is lifted. Add the flour and whisk in. Add the chocolate mixture, a third at a time, whisking briefly between each addition.

4 Pour the mixture into the prepared moulds - it should come almost to the top. Place on a baking tray and cook in the oven for 15-16 minutes. The puddings should be well risen and cracked on top.

5 Remove from the oven and leave for 2 minutes before easing the mixture gently away from the rims using a knife. Invert onto serving plates, dust with icing sugar and serve immediately. Great with vanilla ice cream.

Per serving: 750 cals, 53.5g fat, 33.1g sat fat, 50.3g total sugars, 0.2g salt

Tropical fruit pavlova

Serves 12
Prep time: 20 minutes, plus overnight cooling
Cook time: 1 hour

This impressive dessert is full of fabulous, fresh exotic fruit

4 medium eggs, whites only
230g caster sugar
1 teaspoon white wine vinegar
1 teaspoon cornflour
1 teaspoon vanilla essence
1 x 300ml pot Sainsbury's double cream

1 tablespoon icing sugar, plus a little extra for dusting
½ x mango, peeled, stone removed and sliced
½ x pineapple (about 180g), peeled and chopped
2 kiwi fruit, peeled and sliced
seeds of 2 passionfruit

1 Preheat the oven to 150°C, fan 130°C, gas 2.

2 Draw a 26cm circle on a sheet of baking parchment, then turn over and place on a baking tray.

3 In a grease-free bowl, whisk the egg whites until stiff. Add the caster sugar, a spoonful at a time, continuing to whisk. Once the mixture is shiny and stiff, stir in the white wine vinegar, cornflour and vanilla essence.

4 Spread the mixture onto the baking tray to fill the drawn circle. Lightly push the mixture up at the sides to make sure it creates a dip in the middle once cooked. Bake in the oven for 1 hour, then turn the oven off and leave the pavlova inside to cool for at least 1 hour – for best results, leave in the oven overnight.

5 Whisk the cream with the icing sugar, then spread into the hollow of the cooled pavlova. Decorate with the fruit, dust with icing sugar, then serve.

Per serving: 244 cals, 14.1g fat, 8g sat fat, 25.4g total sugars, trace salt

Time-saving tip
Fill a ready-made pavlova base with cream and tropical fruit instead of making your own meringue

'As good to eat as it looks, this wonderful pud is a great centrepiece'

Makes 6
Prep time: 15 minutes
Cook time: 3 hours

Meringues

Smooth and glossy on the outside, gooey and chewy on the inside, these patisserie-style meringues are heavenly - and easy when you know how

6 medium eggs, whites only	330g caster sugar

1 Preheat the oven to 120°C, fan 100°C, gas ½.

2 In a grease-free glass or stainless-steel bowl, use an electric hand mixer to beat the egg whites until they form stiff peaks. Add the sugar, 1 tablespoon at a time, and continue beating until the meringue mixture is thick and glossy.

3 Line 2 baking sheets with baking parchment. Spoon on the mixture in 6 large dollops. Bake for 2 hours. Turn off the oven and keep in the oven for 1 more hour.

Per serving: 243 cals, trace fat, trace sat fat, 57.8g total sugars, 0.2g salt

Add some flavour...

• Pistachio - stir chopped pistachios or your favourite nuts through the mixture

• Rose - for a rosy hue, stir in a few drops of rose water and a drop of red food colouring

• Chocolate - gently fold cocoa powder or grated chocolate through the mixture

• Lemon - for a citrus twist, add lemon zest and a little yellow food colouring

"These pretty meringues have crisp shells and gorgeous chewy centres"

cookies
& biscuits

Makes 12
Prep time: 15 minutes,
plus chilling and
cooling time
Cook time: 45 minutes

Millionaire's shortbread

Rich and decadent, this melt-in-the-mouth shortbread is one in a million

160g plain flour

60g caster sugar

215g unsalted butter, cut into small pieces

1 x 397g tin condensed milk

100g light brown soft sugar

2 tablespoons golden syrup

150g Sainsbury's Belgian milk chocolate

50g Sainsbury's Belgian white chocolate

1 Preheat the oven to 180°C, fan 160°C, gas 4.

2 In a food processor, whizz the flour, caster sugar and 115g butter until it's like breadcrumbs. Press into an 18cm square tin and prick with a fork. Chill for 20 minutes, then bake for 30 minutes, until just turning golden. Cool in the tin.

3 In a pan, heat the condensed milk, brown sugar, syrup and remaining 100g butter. Bring to the boil, stirring all the time. Boil, still stirring, for 5-8 minutes until thickened. Pour the caramel onto the shortbread, then cool for 30 minutes.

4 Melt the milk and white chocolate separately. Pour the milk chocolate on the caramel, then pour on the white choc. Swirl with a skewer to create a marbled effect. Chill for 2 hours until set, then remove from the tin and cut into squares.

Per serving: 465 cals, 25.5g fat, 11.7g sat fat, 43g total sugars, 0.1g salt

Shortbread

Preheat the oven to 180°C, fan 160°C, gas 4. In a food processor, whizz 160g plain flour, 60g caster sugar and 115g unsalted butter, cubed, until it resembles breadcrumbs. Pat together to form a ball, then roll out on a lightly floured surface, until 0.5cm thick. Cut out rounds with a 7cm pastry cutter and place on a baking tray lined with baking parchment. Sprinkle with 15g demerara sugar, then chill for 20 minutes. Bake for 15 minutes, until just turning golden.

MAKES 20   Prep time: 35 minutes   Cook time: 15 minutes

Each: 87 cals, 4.8g fat, 3.2g sat fat, 4g total sugars, trace salt

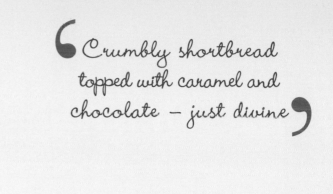

Orange biscotti

These crunchy, twice-baked Italian biscuits, flavoured with orange and pistachio, are delectable dunked in coffee

Makes 30
Prep time: 20 minutes, plus cooling time
Cook time: 50 minutes

200g caster sugar
2 medium eggs
zest of 1 small orange
200g plain flour, sifted, plus extra for dusting

1 teaspoon baking powder
100g pistachios
50g hazelnuts
50g macadamia nuts

1 Preheat the oven to 180°C, fan 160°C, gas 4. Line a baking tray with baking parchment.

2 Using an electric hand mixer, beat together the sugar, eggs and orange zest in a bowl. Stir in the flour, baking powder and nuts, then mix to a sticky dough.

3 Knead the dough on a lightly floured surface until smooth. Using floured hands, divide into 2 portions and roll each into a 30cm log. Bake on the baking tray for 30 minutes or until lightly browned. Cool on the tray for 10 minutes.

4 Reduce the oven temperature to 160°C, fan 140°C, gas 3. Cut the logs into 1cm slices diagonally and place back on the baking tray. Bake for 10 minutes, until golden on top. Turn over and bake for 5-10 minutes. Cool on a wire rack.

Per serving: 102 cals, 4.6g fat, 0.7g sat fat, 7.3g total sugars, trace salt

Viennese fingers

Preheat the oven to 190°C, fan 170°C, gas 5. Cream 100g butter with 25g icing sugar until fluffy. Beat in 100g plain flour, ¼ teaspoon baking powder and 2 drops vanilla extract. Spoon into a piping bag with a large star nozzle. Pipe into 6cm fingers, spaced apart, on 2 baking trays lined with baking parchment. Chill for 30 minutes. Bake for 12 minutes, then cool completely on a wire rack. Dip into 150g melted Belgian dark chocolate. Leave to set on baking parchment.

MAKES 30   Prep time: 45 minutes   Cook time: 12 minutes

Each: 67 cals, 4.4g fat, 2.9g sat fat, 3.3g total sugars, trace salt

Butterscotch cookies

Makes 14
Prep time: 20 minutes, plus cooling time
Cook time: 15 minutes

These delicious cookies have a super-soft centre with chewy butterscotch pieces

100g unsalted butter
100g Sainsbury's Fairtrade light brown soft sugar
1 tablespoon golden syrup

150g Taste the Difference extra fine sponge flour, sifted, plus extra for dusting
50g Sainsbury's mini butterscotch chips

1 Preheat the oven to 180°C, fan 160°C, gas 4. Line a large baking tray with baking parchment.

2 Using an electric hand mixer, beat together the butter and sugar until pale and fluffy. Add the golden syrup and beat for 1 minute. Add the flour and butterscotch chips and mix with a wooden spoon until a soft dough forms.

3 Lightly dust your hands with flour, then divide the dough into 14 balls. Flatten slightly with the palm of your hand and place on the baking tray, leaving space for them to spread out. Bake for 12–15 minutes, until lightly golden at the edges.

4 Remove from the oven and leave to cool on a wire rack.

Per serving: 139 cals, 6.6g fat, 4.2g sat fat, 10.6g total sugars, trace salt

Triple chocolate cookies

Preheat the oven to 180°C, fan 160°C, gas 4. Using an electric mixer, whisk together 150g unsalted butter, 100g light brown soft sugar, 75g caster sugar and 1 teaspoon vanilla extract. Whisk in 150g melted dark chocolate and 1 beaten egg. Beat in 175g plain flour, 2 tablespoons cocoa powder, 1 teaspoon baking powder, a pinch of salt and 150g each milk and white chocolate, in chunks. Spoon rounds onto 2 baking trays lined with baking parchment. Bake for 12 minutes.

MAKES 22 Prep time: 25 minutes   Cook time: 12 minutes

Each: 243 cals, 14.4g fat, 6.6g sat fat, 18.8g total sugars, 0.2g salt

These soft and chewy butterscotch cookies are simply irresistible

Makes 30
Prep time: 20 minutes,
plus cooling time
Cook time: 20 minutes

Florentines

These chewy, chocolate-coated biscuits are full of mouthwatering dried fruits

---

60g unsalted butter
60g light brown soft sugar
1 tablespoon golden syrup
30g plain flour
1 teaspoon mixed spice
40g mixed peel

80g flaked almonds
60g glacé cherries, cut into small pieces
60g crystallised ginger
100g Belgian dark chocolate, chopped
100g Belgian white chocolate, chopped

---

1 Preheat the oven to 180°C, fan 160°C, gas 4. Line 2 baking trays with baking parchment.

2 Melt the butter, sugar and golden syrup in a pan over a low heat. Once the sugar has dissolved, remove from the heat. Stir in the flour, mixed spice, mixed peel, almonds, glacé cherries and crystallised ginger.

3 Drop teaspoonfuls of the mixture onto the baking trays, leaving space between them. Bake for 10 minutes, until golden, then remove from the oven and leave to cool on the baking trays.

4 When the biscuits are cold, melt the dark and white chocolate in separate bowls over simmering water. Dip half the florentines into the dark chocolate and half into the white chocolate, covering each halfway. Place on baking parchment and leave to set.

Per serving: 97 cals, 5.4g fat, 2.6g sat fat, 9.2g total sugars, trace salt

Makes 8
Prep time: 15 minutes,
plus cooling time
Cook time: 14 minutes

Passionfruit melting moments

Melt-in-the-mouth biscuits with a passionfruit-cream filling

170g salted butter, softened
60g icing sugar
170g plain flour, plus extra for dusting
60g cornflour
1 teaspoon vanilla extract

FOR THE FILLING
80g salted butter, softened
80g icing sugar, sifted
the juice of 1 ripe passionfruit (strain in a sieve
to remove the seeds, or add the seeds too)

1 Preheat the oven to 180°C, fan 160°C, gas 4.

2 Beat together the butter and icing sugar until light and fluffy. Add the flour, cornflour and vanilla extract and beat until the mixture just comes together.

3 Using your hands, roll into 16 balls, then flatten into discs. Place on 2 baking trays lined with baking parchment. Using a lightly floured fork, press down gently on the top of each biscuit. Bake for 12-14 minutes or until just starting to brown. Cool on a wire rack.

4 To make the filling, beat together the butter, icing sugar and juice until creamy. Use to sandwich the biscuit halves together.

Per serving: 415 cals, 26g fat, 16.4g sat fat, 19.2g total sugars, 0.5g salt

Nutty cookies

Preheat the oven to 180°C, fan 160°C, gas 4. Cream 150g unsalted butter with 50g light brown soft sugar, 100g caster sugar and 2 teaspoons vanilla extract. Stir in 1 medium egg, 225g plain flour, 1 teaspoon baking powder and 100g smooth peanut butter. Chop 100g blanched hazelnuts and 100g macadamia nuts, and mix in. Drop walnut-sized balls onto 2 baking trays lined with baking parchment, spaced apart, then press down lightly. Bake for 15 minutes.

MAKES 35   Prep time: 25 minutes   Cook time: 15 minutes

Each: 133 cals, 9.2g fat, 3g sat fat, 4.9g total sugars, trace salt

'Gorgeous biscuits filled with luscious passionfruit cream'

Serves 12
Prep time: 15 minutes,
plus cooling time
Cook time: 20 minutes

Sticky apricot flapjacks

These tasty flapjacks use Sainsbury's freefrom ingredients, so make the ideal treat for anyone following a gluten-free diet

60g Sainsbury's freefrom sunflower spread, plus extra for greasing

80g light brown soft sugar

160g Sainsbury's marshmallows

250g ready-to-eat dried apricots, quartered

220g Sainsbury's freefrom pure oats

1 Preheat the oven to 190°C, fan 170°C, gas 5. Line a 20cm square tin with baking parchment.

2 Gently heat the sunflower spread, sugar and marshmallows together in a saucepan, stirring until combined. Add the apricots, then bring to the boil and stir over a medium heat for 5 minutes.

3 Remove from the heat and add the oats. Mix well, then spoon into the tin. Smooth firmly with an oiled spatula.

4 Bake for about 15-20 minutes, until golden brown. Remove from the oven, allow to cool, then cut into bars to serve.

Per serving: 208 cals, 4.6g fat, 1.3g sat fat, 22.7g total sugars, trace salt

Maple syrup flapjacks

Preheat the oven to 180°C, fan 160°C, gas 4. Line a 16 x 25cm tin with baking parchment. Melt 200g butter in a pan over a medium heat. Stir in 100g Sainsbury's pure maple syrup and 150g light brown soft sugar, and simmer until it's mostly dissolved. Remove from the heat and stir in 325g Sainsbury's porridge oats. Spoon into the tin and bake for 25 minutes. Score into bars but allow to cool before slicing.

MAKES 16   Prep time: 10 minutes   Cook time: 30 minutes

Each: 222 cals, 11.9g fat, 7.3g sat fat, 13.3g total sugars, trace salt

Makes 16
Prep time: 20 minutes,
plus chilling, cooling
and decorating time
Cook time: 12 minutes

Name badge cookies

The kids will love to help make these fun biscuits

100g unsalted butter, softened
100g caster sugar
1 teaspoon vanilla extract
1 medium free-range egg
225g plain flour, plus extra for dusting

TO DECORATE
1 x 500g pack Sainsbury's ready to roll soft white icing
1 tablespoon apricot jam, melted
1 x 4-pack Sainsbury's colour writing icing pens (red, yellow, green and black)

1 Preheat the oven to 180°C, fan 160°C, gas 4. Line a baking tray with baking parchment.

2 Beat the butter and sugar in a large bowl until soft and fluffy. Add the vanilla extract, egg and 1 tablespoon flour and beat to combine. Add the remaining flour and beat again. Bring the mixture together into a ball using your hands, then wrap in clingfilm and chill for 1 hour in the fridge.

3 On a lightly floured surface, roll out the dough to a thickness of 0.5cm, then cut into circles with an 8cm round cutter. Place on the baking tray and bake in the oven for 10-12 minutes, until pale golden. Cool on a wire rack.

4 Roll out the icing to a thickness of 0.5cm, then use the same 8cm cutter to cut out icing rounds. Spread some warmed jam over each biscuit and top with the icing circles. Use the icing pens to write on the kids' names or get them to decorate the biscuits themselves.

Per serving: 200 cals, 6.8g fat, 4.3g sat fat, 21.6g total sugars, trace salt

Gingerbread family

Get the children to help make a whole family of gingerbread people

Makes 5 families
Prep time: 20 minutes, plus cooling and decorating time
Cook time: 12 minutes

80g unsalted butter, softened
50g caster sugar
½ teaspoon bicarbonate of soda
60g golden syrup
2 egg yolks

250g plain flour, plus extra for dusting
1 teaspoon ground ginger
1 teaspoon ground cinnamon
1 x set Tu gingerbread family cookie cutters

1 Preheat the oven to 180°C, fan 160°C, gas 4. Line a baking tray with baking parchment.

2 In a bowl, beat together the butter and sugar until creamy, then stir in the bicarbonate of soda, golden syrup and egg yolks. Sift in the flour, ginger and cinnamon and bring the mixture together with your hands.

3 On a lightly floured surface, roll the mixture out to a thickness of 0.5cm. Use the gingerbread cutters to stamp out 5 gingerbread families.

4 Place the biscuits on the baking tray. Bake for 10-12 minutes, then cool on a wire rack before decorating.

Per serving: 102 cals, 4g fat, 2.4g sat fat, 5.2g total sugars, trace salt

How to decorate your gingerbread family

In a small bowl, thoroughly mix 200g icing sugar with 1½ tablespoons water. Spoon the icing into a piping bag with a fine nozzle and draw some hair and clothes on the gingerbread biscuits. Use Sainsbury's 4-pack colour writing icing pens (red, yellow, green and black), Sainsbury's princess sprinkles and Sainsbury's chocolate beans to create faces and add sparkly details.

Makes 20
Prep time: 20 minutes,
plus chilling, cooling
and decorating time
Cook time: 10 minutes

'Thank you' cookies

These pretty cookies make a thoughtful gift for a family member or to thank a teacher at the end of term

100g unsalted butter
100g caster sugar
1 egg yolk, beaten with 2 teaspoons water
1 teaspoon vanilla extract
200g plain flour, plus extra for dusting

TO DECORATE
180g icing sugar, sifted
sprinkles, chocolate beans, chocolate
stars etc

1 In a medium bowl, beat together the butter and sugar until light and creamy. Beat in the egg yolk, vanilla extract, flour and a pinch of salt. Stir until it forms a dough, then knead until smooth. Wrap in clingfilm and chill for 30 minutes.

2 Preheat the oven to 180ºC, fan 160ºC, gas 4.

3 Roll out the dough on a floured surface to a thickness of 0.5cm. Stamp out shapes with cutters and bake on a non-stick baking tray for about 10 minutes, until lightly browned. Cool on a wire rack.

4 Place the icing sugar in a bowl and add cold water, a couple of drops at a time, until the icing has a thick pouring consistency. Spread a little on each cookie and decorate with sprinkles while the icing is wet.

Per serving: 136 cals, 4.5g fat, 2.7g sat fat, 14.8g total sugars, trace salt

For chocolate cookies...
Swap 25g flour for cocoa powder. When icing them, swap 3 tablespoons icing sugar for cocoa powder and mix with warm water

Use a selection of cookie cutters to stamp out different shapes, and decorate with icing and sprinkles for an extra-special gift

'Show someone you care with a gift of homemade goodies'

savoury baking

Makes 12
Prep time: 30 minutes,
plus chilling time
Cook time: 40 minutes

Cheesy ham & asparagus stratas

Stratas are an irresistible combination of fluffy eggs, bread and cheese

30g unsalted butter
1 leek, thinly sliced
1 loaf stale white bread (around 350g), crusts cut off, cut into 2.5cm cubes
110g Cheddar, grated
100g asparagus, blanched, cut into 3cm pieces

110g Taste the Difference British honey roast ham, roughly chopped
5 medium eggs
240ml semi-skimmed milk
1 teaspoon mustard powder
1 teaspoon salt

1 Preheat the oven to 180°C, fan 160°C, gas 4.

2 Melt the butter over a medium heat. Add the leek and cook until soft, then cool.

3 In a large bowl, mix the leek with the bread, cheese, asparagus and ham. Whisk the remaining ingredients in another bowl, then gently fold into the bread mix.

4 Cut squares of baking parchment with pinking shears, and use to line a 12-hole muffin tin. Spoon in the mixture and cover with clingfilm. Chill for 30 minutes, then remove the clingfilm. Bake for 25-30 minutes until golden. Serve warm or cold.

Per serving: 186 cals, 9.3g fat, 4.6g sat fat, 2.8g total sugars, 1.1g salt

Cheese straws

Preheat the oven to 200°C, fan 180°C, gas 6. Rub 125g unsalted butter into 250g plain flour. Stir in a pinch of mustard powder, 50g grated Cheddar and 50g grated Red Leicester. Add 1 egg yolk and a little water, and mix into a firm dough. On a floured board, roll out the pastry into a large rectangle. Cut into straws about ¾cm thick. Brush with beaten egg and dip in poppy seeds. Bake on non-stick baking trays for 15-20 minutes, until golden and crisp.

MAKES 30   Prep time: 10 minutes   Cook time: 20 minutes
Each: 84 cals, 5.4g fat, 3.1g sat fat, 0.1g total sugars, trace salt

Makes 4
Prep time: 15 minutes,
plus chilling time
Cook time: 25 minutes

Tomato tarte tatins

Balsamic and thyme give a delicious twist to these individual tarte tatins

flour, for dusting
1 x 500g pack Sainsbury's puff pastry
2 tablespoons balsamic vinegar
3 tablespoons caster sugar

30g unsalted butter
1 tablespoon chopped fresh thyme leaves
12 Taste the Difference vine-ripened tomatoes

1 Preheat the oven to 220°C, fan 200°C, gas 7.

2 On a floured surface, roll out the pastry to a thickness of 4mm, then cut out 4 circles slightly larger than 10cm tartlet tins. Chill in the fridge for 10 minutes.

3 Meanwhile, heat the balsamic vinegar and sugar in a small saucepan, stirring until the sugar dissolves. Simmer for about 2 minutes, until slightly syrupy. Remove from the heat and add the butter and thyme, stirring until the butter has melted. Divide the sauce between 4 tartlet tins.

4 Place 3 vine tomatoes (tops facing down) into the balsamic caramel in each tin. Top with the pastry circles and gently tuck in the sides.

5 Place the tins on a baking tray and cook for 20 minutes. Allow to rest for 2–3 minutes before inverting each tart onto a plate to serve. Great with a salad.

Per serving: 375 cals, 40.4g fat, 16.3g sat fat, 17.3g total sugars, 1.2g salt

Tomato & Gruyère whirls

Unroll 375g ready-rolled puff pastry and spread with 150g Taste the Difference tomato chutney. Top with 100g Gruyère, grated. Tightly roll up one longer side to the middle. Repeat with the other long edge, to meet in the middle. Wrap in clingfilm and chill for 30 minutes. Preheat the oven to 200°C, fan 180°C, gas 6. Cut the pastry into 1cm slices and place on a baking tray lined with baking parchment. Bake for 15 minutes. Cool on a wire rack.

MAKES 20   Prep time: 45 minutes   Cook time: 15 minutes

Each: 124 cals, 8.7g fat, 3.4g sat fat, 1.8g total sugars, 0.4g salt

"These caramelised tomato tarts make great vegetarian meals"

Serves 6
Prep time: 15 minutes
Cook time: 25 minutes

Wild mushroom tartlets

Mushrooms and crème fraîche make perfect partners in these luxurious little tarts - great as a starter or for lunch

flour, for dusting
1 x 500g pack Sainsbury's puff pastry
2 cloves garlic, peeled
½ teaspoon salt
1 tablespoon olive oil
50g unsalted butter

2 x 140g packs Taste the Difference exotic mushrooms, roughly chopped
½ teaspoon dried thyme
50ml white wine
200ml half-fat crème fraîche
1 egg, beaten
50g pine nuts, toasted

1   Preheat the oven to 220°C, fan 200°C, gas 7.

2   On a lightly floured surface, roll out the pastry into a rectangle, 0.5cm thick, then cut into 6 rectangular pieces. Using a knife, score a border about 1cm inside the edge of each pastry rectangle. Bake for 12 minutes.

3   Meanwhile, crush the garlic and salt into a purée using a pestle and mortar. Mix in the olive oil. Heat the garlic mixture and butter in a large frying pan. Once melted, add the mushrooms and thyme. Sauté for 5-8 minutes, until cooked and softened. Add the wine and bring to the boil, then add half the crème fraîche and bring to the boil again. Remove from the heat.

4   When the pastry cases are cooked, push down the centres. Brush the edges with beaten egg and fill the cases with the mushroom mixture. Turn down the oven temperature to 200°C, fan 180°C, gas 6.

5   Divide the remaining 100ml crème fraîche between the pastry cases, then top with the pine nuts. Bake for a further 8-10 minutes and serve warm. Great with a crisp salad.

Per serving: 523 cals, 42.9g fat, 16.2g sat fat, 2.5g total sugars, 1.3g salt

Serves 4
Prep time: 20 minutes,
plus resting time
Cook time: 40 minutes

Butternut squash, goats' cheese & thyme pizza

This flavour-packed pizza is ideal for an informal weekend meal

1 medium butternut squash, peeled, seeds removed and cut into 2cm chunks
1½ tablespoons olive oil
2 x 125g packs Sainsbury's Abergavenny goats' cheese
1 tablespoon fresh thyme leaves
25g pumpkin seeds

FOR THE PIZZA DOUGH BASE
350g strong plain flour, plus extra for dusting
1½ teaspoons salt
1 x 7g sachet fast action dried yeast
1 tablespoon olive oil

1　Preheat the oven to 200ºC, fan 180ºC, gas 6. Place the squash on a roasting tray, drizzle with 1 tablespoon olive oil and season with salt and freshly ground black pepper. Toss to coat and roast on the lower shelf of the oven for 20-25 minutes. When the squash is tender, remove from the oven and allow to cool slightly.

2　Meanwhile, make the pizza dough. Place the flour, salt, yeast and olive oil in a bowl. Pour in 275ml warm water and mix until fully combined – the dough will be quite soft. Cover with clingfilm and leave for 15 minutes.

3　Remove the dough from the bowl and knead briefly on a floured surface, then place back in the bowl and cover with clingfilm. Leave for a further 10 minutes. Knead again briefly, then roll out into 2 x 25cm circles and place on 2 lightly floured baking trays.

4　Turn up the oven temperature to 220ºC, fan 200ºC, gas 7. Scatter the squash, goats' cheese, thyme leaves and pumpkin seeds over the pizza base. Drizzle with the remaining ½ tablespoon olive oil and season with freshly ground black pepper. Bake for 10-15 minutes.

Per serving: 689 cals, 26.8g fat, 13.1g sat fat, 11.5g total sugars, 3g salt

Serves 6
Prep time: 10 minutes, plus resting time
Cook time: 40 minutes

Roasted pepper tart

Melting goats' cheese and thyme leaves add fantastic flavour to this tart

3 red peppers, deseeded and halved

2 red onions, peeled and sliced into thin wedges

2½ tablespoons olive oil, plus extra for greasing

375g ready-rolled puff pastry

1 large egg, beaten

150g goats' cheese, thinly sliced

1 teaspoon fresh thyme leaves

1 Grill the peppers on high for 5–8 minutes, turning frequently, until blackened. Place in a bowl and cover with clingfilm for 15–20 minutes, until cool. Remove the skin, wash off any residue, then slice the peppers into strips.

2 Preheat the oven to 200°C, fan 180°C, gas 6. In a pan, gently cook the onion in 1 tablespoon oil for 8–10 minutes. Turn up the heat, add the peppers and cook for 5 minutes. Remove from the heat.

3 Unroll the pastry on a lightly greased baking sheet. Using a sharp knife, gently score a border 2cm from the edge of the pastry. Brush the border with the egg. Spoon the peppers and onion onto the pastry, keeping within the border.

4 Place the cheese on top and sprinkle on the thyme. Drizzle over the remaining 1½ tablespoons oil. Cook for 15 minutes, until the pastry is puffed up and the cheese is melting.

Per serving: 495 cals, 35.3g fat, 13.5g sat fat, 8.3g total sugars, 1.2g salt

Tomato & asparagus tarts

Preheat the oven to 220°C, fan 200°C, gas 7. Unroll 1 x 375g sheet ready-rolled puff pastry and cut into 8 squares. Score a border 1cm inside the edge of each square, then bake for 15 minutes. Push down the centre of each square. Brush the centres with some green pesto and top each with 2 asparagus spears, halved lengthways, and a slice of tomato. Sprinkle with Parmigiano Reggiano and bake for 5–8 minutes, until golden. Garnish with washed rocket leaves.

SERVES 8   Prep time: 10 minutes   Cook time: 25 minutes

Each: 337 cals, 24.9g fat, 6.8g sat fat, 2.3g total sugars, 0.7g salt

Cornish pasties

Makes 4
(each serves 2)
Prep time: 20 minutes,
plus chilling time
Cook time: 55 minutes

Packed with steak and seasoned veg, each pasty is big enough to serve two

500g plain flour
125g butter, diced
125g lard, diced
1 tablespoon sunflower oil
1 onion, peeled and chopped

150g swede, peeled and cut into 1cm dice
150g potato, peeled and cut into 1cm dice
100g carrot, peeled and cut into 1cm dice
350g sirloin steak, cut into very small pieces
1 egg, beaten

1   Rub together the flour, butter and lard until it resembles breadcrumbs. Add about 5 tablespoons ice-cold water and mix to a firm dough. Cover with clingfilm and chill in the fridge for 20 minutes.

2   Heat the oil in a pan and cook the onion for 6 minutes. Tip into a bowl and add the swede, potato and carrot. Season well with salt and ground black pepper.

3   Preheat the oven to 200°C, fan 180°C, gas 6. Roll out the pastry and cut out 4 circles around a 20cm plate. Place a quarter of the veg mix on one half of each circle and top with the steak. Brush the edges with egg. Fold the pastry over the filling and crimp the edges with your fingers. Place on a baking tray lined with baking parchment. Brush with egg and chill for 15 minutes. Bake for 10 minutes. Reduce the temperature to 180°C, fan 160°C, gas 4 and bake for 40 minutes.

Per serving: 439 cals, 23.7g fat, 11.1g sat fat, 3.7g total sugars, 0.4g salt

Mini Gruyère & thyme scones

Preheat the oven to 200°C, fan 180°C, gas 6. Sift 225g strong white bread flour, 1 tablespoon baking powder and a pinch of salt into a bowl. Rub in 40g butter. Stir in 80g grated Gruyère, 1 teaspoon Dijon mustard, some fresh thyme leaves and 1 teaspoon cayenne pepper. Gradually add 150ml milk, mixing with a knife to form a dough. Roll out until 2cm thick. Cut out rounds with a 5cm pastry cutter and sprinkle with 45g grated Gruyère. Bake for 12-15 minutes on a greased baking tray.

MAKES 15   Prep time: 15 minutes   Cook time: 15 minutes

Each: 113 cals, 5.4g fat, 3g sat fat, 0.8g total sugars, 0.4g salt

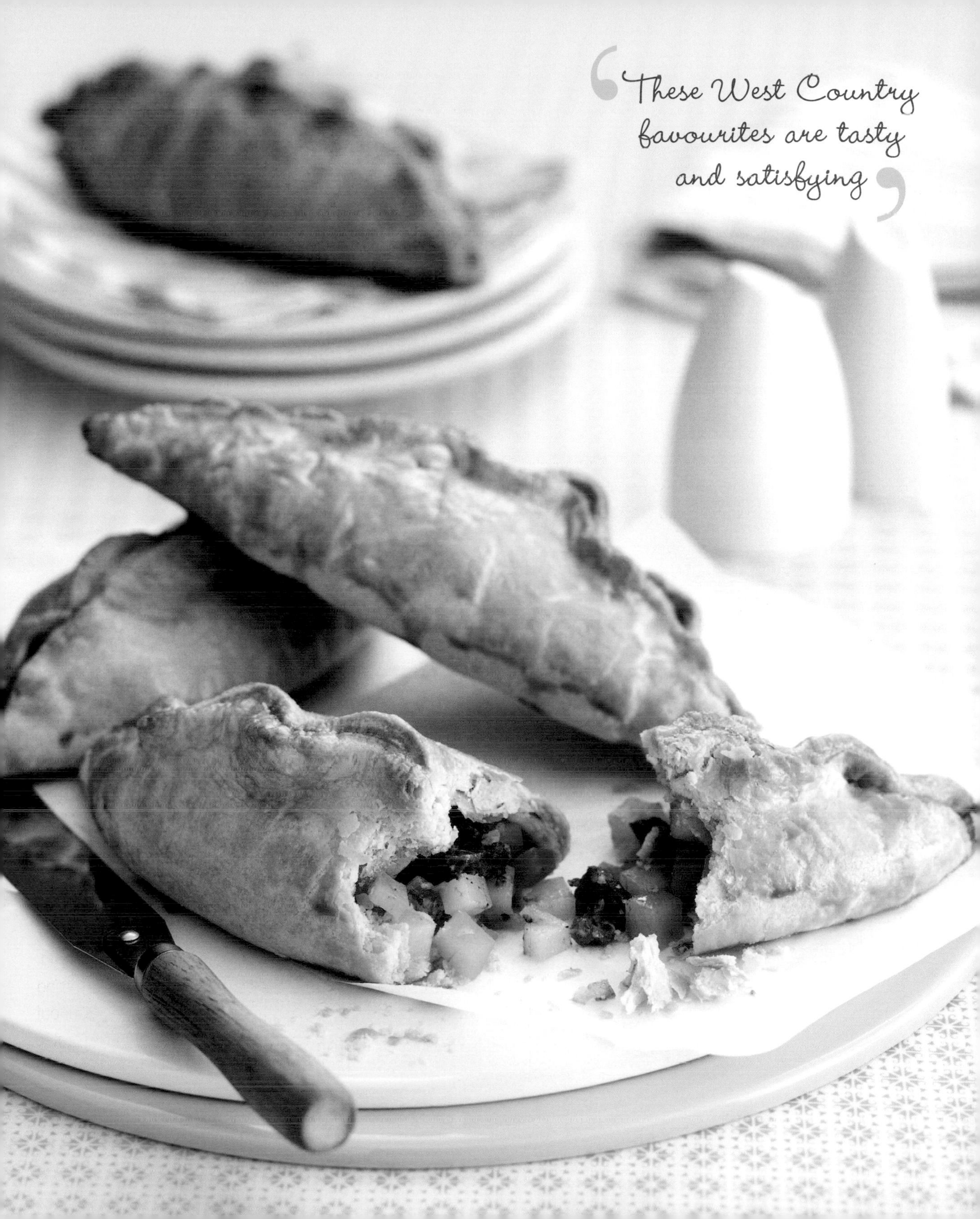

"These West Country favourites are tasty and satisfying"

Serves 6
Prep time: 10 minutes,
plus cooling time
Cook time: 45 minutes

Smoked trout, leek & pea quiche

This savoury quiche is sure to be a winner with the whole family – you can also make it with smoked salmon

flour, for dusting
½ x 500g pack Sainsbury's shortcrust pastry
25g unsalted butter
1 medium leek, trimmed, washed and finely chopped
75g frozen peas

½ x 300ml pot Sainsbury's half fat crème fraîche
2 large eggs, beaten
3 tablespoons whole milk
1 x 120g pack Sainsbury's smoked trout, flaked
rocket leaves, to garnish

1 Preheat the oven to 200°C, fan 180°C, gas 6.

2 Roll the pastry out on a lightly floured surface and use to line a 20cm round tart tin, then chill in the fridge for 20 minutes.

3 Remove the pastry case from the fridge, top with a sheet of baking parchment and fill with baking beans or uncooked rice. Bake for 10 minutes. Remove the beans and baking parchment and cook for another 5 minutes.

4 Meanwhile, heat the butter in a pan. Add the leek and cook, stirring occasionally, for 5–8 minutes until softened. Stir in the peas and remove from the heat.

5 Lower the oven temperature to 180°C, fan 160°C, gas 4. Mix together the crème fraîche, eggs and milk. Season with freshly ground black pepper.

6 Place the leek and peas in the bottom of the part-cooked pastry case, then top with pieces of smoked trout. Carefully pour over the egg mixture, then bake for 25–30 minutes, until the filling has set. Allow to cool slightly before garnishing with rocket leaves.

Per serving: 366 cals, 24.6g fat, 14.5g sat fat, 3.6g total sugars, 1g salt

Did you know...?
Sainsbury's specially selected fresh rainbow trout are smoked using oak and beech chippings for a wonderfully smooth, smoky flavour

breads

Makes 1 loaf (8 slices)
Prep time: 15 minutes,
plus proving time
Cook time: 25 minutes

Olive & rosemary focaccia

This flavoursome Italian flatbread looks charmingly rustic – and as it's made using a bread mix, it's really easy, too

1 x 500g pack Sainsbury's crusty white bread mix
1 x 180g pack Sainsbury's olives in a chilli & garlic dressing (or pitted olives of your choice)

oil, for greasing
½ x 20g pack Sainsbury's rosemary, stalks removed and broken into sprigs

1 Make up the dough following pack instructions and allow to prove for the recommended time.

2 Reserving the dressing, stone the olives and roughly chop.

3 Preheat the oven to 220°C, fan 200°C, gas 7.

4 Knead half the olives into the dough and roll out to a rough oval shape, about 3cm thick. Place on a lightly oiled baking tray and make indentations all over in the dough by pressing with the tips of your fingers. Stud the dough with rosemary sprigs, then cover with a damp tea towel or oiled clingfilm and set aside for another 20 minutes to prove.

5 Sprinkle with the remaining chopped olives and cook in the oven for 20-25 minutes, until golden brown. Drizzle the bread with the dressing from the olives before serving.

Per slice: 192 cals, 4.9g fat, 0.9g sat fat, 1.6g total sugars, 1.3g salt

This fantastic textured bread is full of Italian flavours

Makes 1 loaf (8 slices)
Prep time: 10 minutes,
plus proving time
Cook time: 55 minutes

Multigrain loaf

Everyone is sure to love the taste, texture and aroma of home-baked bread, and the oats and seeds give this multigrain loaf extra bite

---

525g wholemeal bread flour
25g oats, roughly chopped (optional – if omitted, increase flour to 550g)
1 teaspoon salt
1 tablespoon sesame seeds

1 tablespoon poppy seeds
2 tablespoons sunflower seeds
1 x 7g sachet fast action dried yeast
1 tablespoon black treacle
½ teaspoon oil, for greasing

---

1 Sift the flour, oats (if using) and salt into a large bowl. Mix together all the seeds in another bowl. Stir three-quarters of the seeds into the flour mixture and mix well.

2 Mix the yeast and treacle in a jug with 100ml warm water. Allow to foam for 5 minutes.

3 Stir the yeast mixture into the flour mixture along with about 400ml warm water and mix thoroughly until combined into a smooth, wettish dough.

4 Oil a 2lb loaf tin, then tip in the dough. Cover with a damp tea towel and set aside to rest until slightly risen (about 20 minutes). Preheat the oven to 230°C, fan 210°C, gas 8.

5 Sprinkle the dough with water, then scatter on the remaining seeds. Cook in the oven for 20 minutes, then reduce the temperature to 200°C, fan 180°C, gas 6 and cook for a further 30–35 minutes. The loaf is ready when it has browned and sounds hollow when tapped on the base.

Per slice: 285 cals, 5.2g fat, 0.8g sat fat, 2.9g total sugars, 0.6g salt

"Imagine the aroma of home-baked bread wafting through the house..."

Makes 1 loaf (8 slices)
Prep time: 15 minutes,
plus proving time
Cook time: 20 minutes

Red onion focaccia

This incredibly easy, fragrant bread would make a delicious snack or starter

---

1 x 500g pack Sainsbury's sunflower
speciality brown bread mix
2 red onions, peeled and finely sliced

2 tablespoons fresh parsley, chopped
1 tablespoon olive oil, plus extra for greasing

---

1 Prepare the bread mix following pack instructions, until step 4. Shape the bread into a rectangle (about 22 x 30cm), then place on a greased baking tray and leave to rest until doubled in size (about 1 hour).

2 Preheat the oven to 200°C, fan 180°C, gas 6.

3 Once the bread has risen, push deep holes into the dough using an oiled finger. Scatter the onion and parsley over, then season with salt and freshly ground black pepper. Drizzle with the olive oil, making sure some goes into the holes.

4 Bake for 20 minutes, until the bread springs back when touched, then serve.

Per slice: 193 cals, 5.4g fat, 1g sat fat, 2.6g total sugars, 0.8g salt

"Red onion and parsley add extra flavour to this easy bread"

Makes 1 loaf (8 slices)
Prep time: 25 minutes,
plus proving time
Cook time: 30 minutes

Cottage loaf

This hearty, country-style loaf is a fantastic way to enjoy home-made bread

400g strong bread flour, plus extra for dusting	1 x 7g sachet fast action dried yeast
½ teaspoon salt	½ teaspoon oil, for greasing
50g unsalted butter, softened	1 egg, beaten with 1 teaspoon water
250ml semi-skimmed milk or water, warmed	25g poppy seeds or sesame seeds

1 Place the flour and salt in a large bowl and mix well. Rub in the butter, using your fingertips. Pour the milk or water into another bowl, then sprinkle on the yeast. Allow to foam for 5 minutes, then stir into the flour to form a soft dough.

2 Turn the dough out onto a floured surface and knead for 5-10 minutes, until smooth. Place in a lightly oiled bowl, cover with oiled clingfilm and leave in a warm place for 1 hour to prove.

3 Turn out the dough onto a floured surface and knead again for about 5 minutes, until smooth. Cut off a third of the dough and shape into a ball, then set aside. Shape the remaining dough into a ball and place on a greased baking tray. Top with the smaller dough ball and press down slightly.

4 Use a floured finger to push down through the centre of the loaf, from the top to the bottom. Cover with oiled clingfilm and leave in a warm place for 30 minutes to prove.

5 Preheat the oven to 220°C, fan 200°C, gas 7. Brush the loaf with a little of the egg and water mixture, sprinkle with poppy or sesame seeds, and bake for 10 minutes. Reduce the oven temperature to 200°C, fan 180°C, gas 6 and bake for 15-20 minutes. The loaf is ready when it's golden brown and sounds hollow when tapped on the base. Transfer to a wire rack to cool.

Per slice: 266 cals, 8.9g fat, 4g sat fat, 2.3g total sugars, 0.4g salt

Time-saving tip
Knead the dough in a food processor with a dough hook
if you have one – it makes this loaf quick and easy

Makes 1 loaf (8 slices)
Prep time: 20 minutes
Cook time: 30 minutes

Soda bread

This no-fuss soda bread is ideal when you're in a hurry, as it contains no yeast and needs no proving time

250g plain flour, plus extra for dusting
250g wholemeal flour
1 teaspoon salt
1 teaspoon bicarbonate of soda
1 teaspoon cream of tartar

1 teaspoon caster sugar
25g unsalted butter
1 x 284ml pot Sainsbury's cultured buttermilk
100–150ml semi-skimmed milk

1   Preheat the oven to 190ºC, fan 170ºC, gas 5.

2   Place the plain flour, wholemeal flour, salt, bicarbonate of soda, cream of tartar and sugar in a bowl. Add the butter and rub in with your fingertips.

3   Stir in the buttermilk and enough milk (start with 100ml) to mix to a stiff consistency, taking care not to over-mix. Knead very lightly and shape into a ball.

4   Place the dough on a lightly floured baking tray. Cut a 1-inch deep cross in the centre and bake in the oven for 25–30 minutes until risen, golden brown and the centre of the cross feels firm. Remove from the oven and wrap in a clean tea towel to cool. This bread is best eaten on the day of making, but will also be good toasted the day after.

Per slice: 283 cals, 4.1g fat, 2.6g sat fat, 6.1g total sugars, 1.1g salt

'The wholemeal flour gives this soda bread a delicious coarse texture'

special occasions

Serves 12 children
Prep time: 45 minutes,
plus cooling time
Cook time: 45 minutes

Treasure chest

Shiver me timbers – little pirates will love this treasure trove of goodies

1 ½ tablespoons cocoa powder
4 tablespoons milk
125g unsalted butter, softened
125g Sainsbury's Fairtrade golden caster sugar
2 large eggs
125g self-raising flour
½ teaspoon vanilla extract
1 tablespoon golden syrup

60g caster sugar
100g dark chocolate, broken into small pieces

TO DECORATE
75g Sainsbury's chocolate crispies
2 liquorice Catherine wheels, unwound
liquorice allsorts, chocolate coins and sweets
cocktail sticks

1 Preheat the oven to 180°C, fan 160°C, gas 4. Grease a 1lb loaf tin and line with baking parchment.

2 Mix the cocoa powder with 2 tablespoons milk and set aside. Beat the butter and golden caster sugar together until light and creamy. Add the eggs, one at a time, mixing well after each addition. Fold in the flour and stir through the vanilla and remaining 2 tablespoons milk until the mixture is smooth.

3 Spoon half the mixture into another bowl and stir in the cocoa mixture. Place alternate spoonfuls of each mixture into the loaf tin and drag a skewer through a few times to create a marbled effect. Bake for 30 minutes, then cover with foil if necessary and bake for a further 10 minutes or until a skewer inserted into the cake comes out clean. Leave to cool.

4 For the ganache, heat the syrup, caster sugar and 2 tablespoons water in a pan, stirring occasionally. Once dissolved, bring to the boil then remove from the heat. Add the chocolate and leave to melt, then stir until glossy and thick.

5 Cut the cake in half horizontally, about a third from the top, and cover with ganache. Pour the crispies on a plate and dunk in the cake to decorate all over. Arrange the liquorice 'bands' and place sweets on the bottom cake layer. Add the lid of the chest and secure with cocktail sticks to create a hinged effect.

Per serving: 313 cals, 15.9g fat, 9.2g sat fat, 27.3g total sugars, 0.2g salt

Time-saving tip
For a no-bake option, decorate a Sainsbury's marble cake

This pirate's chest is packed full of special birthday treasure

Fun-filled fort

Serves 30 children
Prep time: 45 minutes, plus cooling time
Cook time: 1 hour, 5 minutes

They'll be king of the castle on their birthday with this colourful chocolate fort

450g self-raising flour
3 teaspoons baking powder
600g caster sugar
125g cocoa, mixed with 300ml boiling water
6 medium eggs, beaten with 120ml water
80ml sunflower oil, plus extra for greasing
350g unsalted butter, melted

TO DECORATE
250g unsalted butter, softened
600g icing sugar, sifted
4 tablespoons cocoa powder
1 teaspoon vanilla extract
6 x 8-pack Sainsbury's Double Take biscuits
5 x 40g tubes Smarties
1 x pack Dr Oetker birthday candles

1 Preheat the oven to 180°C, fan 160°C, gas 4. Grease a 20cm square cake tin and a 1lb loaf tin and line both with baking parchment.

2 In a large bowl, mix together the flour, baking powder and caster sugar. Stir in the cocoa and egg mixtures. Add the sunflower oil and melted butter, then stir well until combined. Half-fill the loaf tin with the mixture and bake for 30–35 minutes. Pour the rest into the square tin and bake for 60–65 minutes. The cakes will be ready when a skewer inserted into them comes out clean. Cool on a wire rack.

3 For the icing, use an electric hand mixer to cream the butter in a bowl. Add the icing sugar, spoon by spoon. Mix the cocoa, vanilla extract and 2–3 tablespoons boiling water to make a thick paste, then beat into the buttercream.

4 Trim the cakes to create an even surface. Trim the edges of the loaf to make a brick shape, then cut in half vertically. Use some of the buttercream to sandwich the halves together vertically to make a tower.

5 Halve the large cake horizontally and sandwich with some more buttercream. Using a palette knife, coat the large cake in buttercream. Place the smaller cake in the centre on top and coat smoothly in buttercream.

6 Stick the chocolate biscuits side by side all around the top tower. Place biscuits at each corner of the base to create turrets, then cut the remaining biscuits to the height of the cake and place around the base. Tip the Smarties onto the tower and around its base.

Per serving: 630 cals, 32.2g fat, 18.7g sat fat, 61.8g total sugars, 0.4g salt

'Prepare for a storming of the castle when they clap eyes on this beauty'

Serves 20 children
Prep time: 45 minutes,
plus cooling time
Cook time: 45 minutes

Loveable lion

This fantastic lion cake will get a roar of approval at the birthday party

75g cocoa powder
4 medium eggs
1 teaspoon vanilla extract
300g self-raising flour
2 teaspoons baking powder
400g caster sugar
50ml sunflower oil
250g unsalted butter, softened, plus extra
for greasing

TO DECORATE
200g unsalted butter
400g icing sugar
1 x 100g pack Sainsbury's mini fudge chunks
2 tablespoons semi-skimmed milk
Sainsbury's caramel & chocolate flavour
writing icing pens
1 x 100g pack Sainsbury's mini honeycomb
pieces
1 x 70g pack Sainsbury's milk chocolate buttons

1 Preheat the oven to 180°C, fan 160°C, gas 4. Grease 2 x 23cm round cake
   tins and line with baking parchment.

2 In a bowl, mix the cocoa powder with 200ml boiling water and stir until
   smooth. In a separate bowl, whisk the eggs with the vanilla extract and
   90ml water until combined, then set aside.

3 In another bowl, sift the flour with the baking powder and caster sugar.
   Add the cocoa mixture and the oil and butter. Beat for 1 minute using an
   electric hand mixer. Gradually add the egg mixture, whisking well after
   each addition. Divide the mixture between the 2 cake tins. Bake for
   40–45 minutes, or until a skewer inserted into the cakes comes out clean.
   Leave to cool in the tins for 10 minutes, then cool completely on a wire rack.

4 For the icing, beat the butter and icing sugar together until light and fluffy.
   In a pan, gently melt the fudge chunks with the milk. Cool slightly then
   beat into the buttercream. Use to sandwich the cakes together and thickly
   coat the top and sides. Using the icing pens, pipe lines outwards from
   halfway, then drag the buttercream outwards with a fork to create a mane.

5 Place the honeycomb pieces in an oval shape in the centre of the cake.
   Decorate with the buttons and icing pens to make whiskers and a face.
   Dot the remaining buttons around the base of the cake.

Per serving: 509 cals, 26.3g fat, 14.6g sat fat, 51.3g total sugars, 0.4g salt

Who could resist a slice of the coolest cat in town?

Serves 25 children
Prep time: 1 hour, plus cooling time
Cook time: 30 minutes

Happy bunny

This rascally rabbit is surprisingly easy to make out of two round cakes

250g unsalted butter, softened
250g caster sugar
4 medium eggs, beaten
250g self-raising flour, sifted

TO DECORATE
125g unsalted butter, softened
250g icing sugar

2 tablespoons semi-skimmed milk
750g ready to roll white icing
25g Sainsbury's pink glimmer sugar
30g Sainsbury's red, white and blue sugar balls
5 Sainsbury's marshmallows
2 Sainsbury's strawberry bon bons
1 x black writing icing pen

1 Preheat the oven to 180°C, fan 160°C, gas 4. Grease 2 x 15cm round cake tins and line with baking parchment.

2 Using an electric hand mixer, beat the butter and caster sugar together until light and fluffy. Slowly add the eggs, a little at a time, beating well after each addition, then fold through the flour. Divide between the 2 cake tins and bake for 30 minutes, or until a skewer inserted into the cakes comes out clean. Leave to cool in their tins for 10 minutes then transfer to a wire rack.

3 To make the ears, cut equal-sized, ear-shaped pieces of sponge away from the sides of one of the cakes (see diagram, right). The remaining sponge will form the bow tie.

left ear
bow tie
right ear

4 Remove 1 pointy end from each cake ear and fit the ears snugly to the second cake. To make the buttercream, beat the butter with the icing sugar and milk until light and fluffy. Cover all the cake and the bow tie in buttercream.

5 Roll out 500g icing into a large circle and smooth it over the face and ears. Cut the icing between the ears and push down the sides. Pinch the excess icing together at the base of the face and at the top of the ears and trim with a knife. Roll out 250g icing and cover the bow tie. Use trimmings for the bow tie detail.

6 Brush a little water over the ears and sprinkle on the glimmer sugar. Brush the bow tie with a little water and cover with coloured sugar balls. Use the marshmallows, bon bons and black writing icing pen to make the face.

Per serving: 379 cals, 15.4g fat, 9.8g sat fat, 50.1g total sugars, 0.2g salt

Serves 20 children
Prep time: 40 minutes,
plus cooling time
Cook time: 40 minutes

Flower power cake

Make her feel like a princess with this gorgeous girly birthday cake

500g unsalted butter, softened
500g caster sugar
2 teaspoons vanilla extract
8 medium eggs
500g self-raising flour
2–3 drops of pink food colouring
10 tablespoons strawberry jam

TO DECORATE
250g unsalted butter, softened
600g icing sugar
3–4 tablespoons milk
a few drops each of pink and green
food colouring
2 x pack Dr Oetker wafer daisies
1 x Sainsbury's non-edible 'happy birthday'
cake decoration
cake candles

1 Preheat the oven to 180°C, fan 160°C, gas 4. Grease 3 x 15cm round springform cake tins and line with baking parchment.

2 Using an electric hand mixer, beat together the butter, sugar and vanilla extract until light and fluffy. Beat in the eggs, one at a time, adding 1 tablespoon flour with each egg. Fold through the remaining flour until fully combined.

3 Pour one-third of the mixture into a bowl. Add a few drops of the pink food colouring and stir well. Pour into a cake tin and divide the remaining cake mixture equally between the 2 remaining tins. Bake for 35–40 minutes, then cool on a wire rack.

4 Trim off the tops of the cakes to create a flat surface, then sandwich together with the jam, with the pink cake in the middle.

5 To make the buttercream icing, whisk together the butter, icing sugar and milk. Place a quarter of the icing in a separate bowl and stir in the green food colouring. Add the pink colouring to the remaining icing.

6 Spread the pink icing over the sides and top of the cake. Spoon the green icing into a piping bag with a small, plain nozzle, then pipe green stalks up the sides of the cake. Arrange the daisy decorations on top and add the birthday plaque and candles.

Per serving: 646 cals, 33.6g fat, 21.1g sat fat, 62g total sugars, 0.3g salt

"This pretty flower cake will make the birthday girl feel extra special"

Serves 16 children
Prep time: 35 minutes,
plus cooling time
Cook time: 35 minutes

Eric the elephant cake

Kids will love this cake inspired by Eric the elephant

250g unsalted butter, plus extra for greasing
250g caster sugar
1 teaspoon vanilla extract
4 medium eggs, lightly beaten
250g self-raising flour, sifted
2 tablespoons semi-skimmed milk

TO DECORATE
150g unsalted butter, softened
200g icing sugar
2 tablespoons semi-skimmed milk
500g Sainsbury's ready to roll white icing
1 tablespoon green food colouring
1 x 75g pack Sainsbury's Eric & Friends fruit gums

1 Preheat the oven to 180°C, fan 160°C, gas 4. Grease 2 x 20cm round cake tins, then line the base of each with baking parchment.

2 Using an electric hand mixer, cream the butter and sugar together until light and fluffy. Add the vanilla extract and the eggs, a little at a time, beating well between each addition. Fold in the flour and add the milk to bring the mixture to a dropping consistency.

3 Divide the mixture between the 2 tins and bake for 30-35 minutes, until well risen and golden. Leave the cakes to cool slightly in their tins, then remove the liners and transfer to a wire rack to cool completely.

4 To make the buttercream, beat the butter with the icing sugar and milk, until light and fluffy. Sandwich the cakes together with half the buttercream, then place on a stand or board. Trim the top cake to create a flat surface, then spread a very thin layer of the buttercream all over the cake.

5 Roll out the icing to make a 30cm circle. Drape over the cake and smooth down, removing any air bubbles. Carefully trim the excess icing from the cake. Add the food colouring to the remaining buttercream and spoon into a piping bag with a small, plain nozzle. Pipe 'grass' around the bottom and on top of the cake and, once set, stick on the fruit gums with a little buttercream.

Per serving: 521 cals, 24.3g fat, 14.7g sat fat, 59.3g total sugars, 0.3g salt

“Decorating this Eric the elephant cake is a walk in the park”

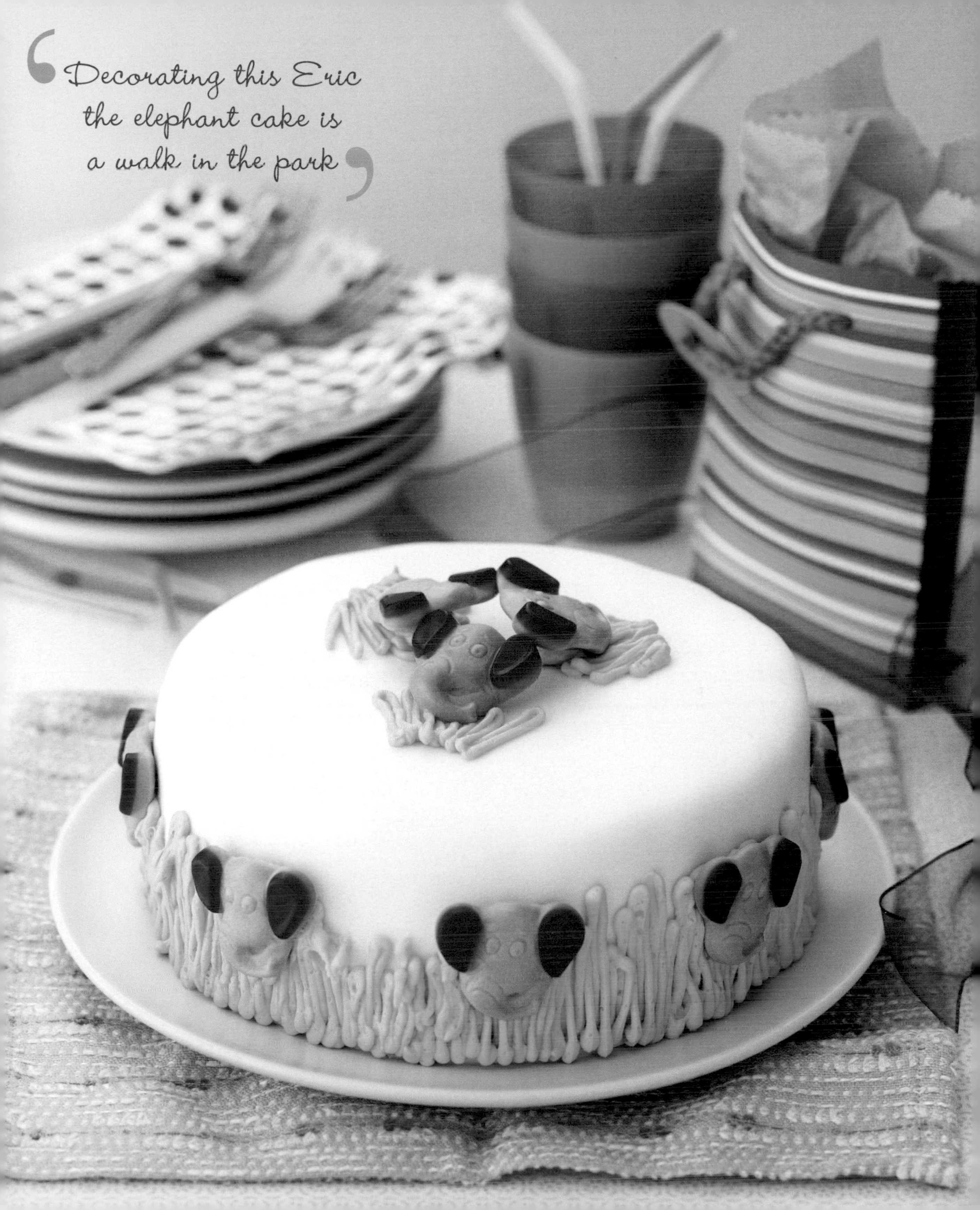

Makes 18
Prep time: 25 minutes,
plus cooling time
Cook time: 14 minutes

Red velvet whoopie pies

Originating in New England, whoopie pies are the latest baking craze. They're chewy and slightly soft, and these red velvet ones are ideal for Valentine's Day

75g unsalted butter, softened
125g light brown soft sugar
1 medium egg
1 teaspoon vanilla extract
1/2 teaspoon baking powder
175g plain flour
50ml buttermilk

1 tablespoon red food colouring

FOR THE ICING
50g cream cheese
30g unsalted butter, softened
1/2 teaspoon vanilla extract
225g icing sugar, sifted, plus extra for dusting

1 Preheat the oven to 180°C, fan 160°C, gas 4. Line 2 baking trays with baking parchment.

2 Beat together the butter and sugar using an electric hand mixer for 2-3 minutes, until light and fluffy. Add the egg and vanilla extract and beat until well combined. Add the baking powder. Whisk in the flour and buttermilk in alternate batches on a low speed, starting and finishing with the flour – be careful not to over-beat. Whisk in the food colouring and a pinch of salt.

3 Spoon the batter into a piping bag fitted with a 1cm plain nozzle. Pipe the batter onto the baking parchment in small circles, about 2-3cm in diameter. Leave a 3cm gap between each as they will spread.

4 Bake for 14 minutes, or until they're puffed up and spring back on touching. Cool on the baking trays for at least 10 minutes, then transfer to a wire rack.

5 For the icing, beat the cream cheese and butter using an electric hand mixer. Add the vanilla extract and icing sugar. Beat on a low speed at first and increase the speed until the icing is smooth and fluffy. Use the icing to sandwich the pies together in pairs, with the flat sides facing each other. Dust with icing sugar before serving.

Per serving: 173 cals, 20.3g fat, 6g sat fat, 3.5g total sugars, 0.2g salt

Makes 50
Prep time: 20 minutes,
plus chilling time
Cook time: 15 minutes

Easter bunny biscuits

This all-in-one biscuit mixture is so easy. Just throw everything into a bowl and get mixing

200g unsalted butter, cut into small cubes
200g caster sugar
1 medium egg, beaten
400g plain flour, plus extra for dusting
2 teaspoons vanilla extract

TO DECORATE
180g icing sugar, sifted
2 tablespoons whole milk
a few drops of pink food colouring
25 mini marshmallows, halved

1 Using an electric hand mixer, beat the butter and sugar together in a bowl, until pale and fluffy. Add the egg and continue to beat. Sift in the flour, then add the vanilla extract and fold through to form a dough.

2 Turn out the dough onto a lightly floured surface and knead gently until smooth. Chill in the fridge for 30 minutes.

3 Remove the dough from the fridge and roll out until it's about 4mm thick.

4 Preheat the oven to 180°C, fan 160°C, gas 4. Line 2 baking trays with baking parchment.

5 Use a 7cm bunny-shaped biscuit cutter to cut biscuits from the dough. Arrange on the baking trays and bake for 12-15 minutes, until golden. Remove from the oven and leave the biscuits on the trays to cool slightly before transferring to wire racks to cool completely.

6 To make the icing, combine the icing sugar, milk and food colouring in a bowl until smooth. Carefully spread over the biscuits and press a marshmallow tail on each.

Per serving: 94 cals, 3.5g fat, 2.2g sat fat, 8.3g total sugars, trace salt

Makes 12
Prep time: 15 minutes,
plus chilling time
Cook time: 10 minutes

Easter pastel flower biscuits

Here's one just for the adults, but you can easily use water instead of Cointreau, if preferred

50g unsalted butter
30g icing sugar, sifted, plus extra for dusting
60g plain flour
25g ground almonds
1 medium egg yolk

FOR THE FILLING
50g unsalted butter
100g icing sugar, sifted, plus extra for dusting
a few drops each of pink and green food colouring
3 teaspoons Cointreau (optional) or water

1 Using an electric hand mixer, beat together 50g butter and 30g icing sugar until creamy. Fold in the flour and almonds, then beat in the egg yolk. Use a palette knife to bring the dough together, then shape it into a ball with your hands. Wrap the dough in clingfilm and chill in the fridge for 20-30 minutes.

2 Preheat the oven to 180°C, fan 160°C, gas 4. Line a baking tray with baking parchment.

3 On a surface dusted with icing sugar, roll out the dough to a thickness of 0.5cm. Cut out 24 flower-shaped biscuits (or you could use a flower-shaped stencil or cutter). Place on the baking tray and cook for 5-10 minutes. Leave to cool.

4 For the filling, beat together the butter and icing sugar. Divide between 2 small bowls and drop a small amount of pink food colouring into one bowl and green colouring into the other. Stir $1\frac{1}{2}$ teaspoons Cointreau (or water, if using) into each bowl.

5 Sandwich half the biscuits together with pink icing, and half with green icing. Dust both sides with icing sugar before serving.

Per serving: 144 cals, 8.5g fat, 4.7g sat fat, 11.4g total sugars, trace salt

Happy Easter

Makes 16
Prep time: 20 minutes,
plus proving time
Cook time: 20 minutes

Hot cross buns

You can't beat the taste and aroma of home-baked hot cross buns at Easter

175g Sainsbury's mixed dried fruit
zest of 1 orange
1 x 7g sachet fast action dried yeast
175g caster sugar
300ml semi-skimmed milk, warmed
600g strong white bread flour
3 teaspoons mixed spice

½ teaspoon ground cinnamon
a good grating of nutmeg
75g unsalted butter, softened, plus
1 tablespoon melted butter
1 egg yolk, mixed with 1 tablespoon milk
50g plain flour

1 Mix the dried fruit and zest in a bowl and set aside. Place the yeast in a jug with 15g caster sugar. Pour over 4 tablespoons warm milk and allow to foam for 5 minutes.

2 In a food processor, pulse the bread flour, 110g caster sugar, a pinch of salt, mixed spice, cinnamon, nutmeg and softened butter, until it resembles breadcrumbs. Tip into a large bowl and make a well in the centre. Pour in the yeast and most of the remaining milk. Mix into a sticky dough, adding more milk if needed. Knead for 8–10 minutes, until smooth and elastic (an electric mixer makes this easy). Knead in the dried fruits and cover with oiled clingfilm. Leave in a warm place to rise for 1 hour, until doubled in size.

3 Press the dough into a rectangular shape. Divide and shape into 16 equal balls. Place, almost touching, on baking trays lined with baking parchment. Cover with a damp tea towel and leave in a warm place until doubled in size and joined together – this may take up to 1 hour, depending on the temperature.

4 Preheat the oven to 230°C, fan 210°C, gas 8. Gently brush the buns with the egg yolk and milk mixture.

5 Mix the plain flour and melted butter with 4 tablespoons water to form a paste. Spoon into a piping bag with a plain nozzle and pipe a cross on each bun. Bake for 5 minutes, then reduce the oven temperature to 190°C, fan 170°C, gas 5 and cook for 10-15 minutes, until golden. Cool on a wire rack.

6 Gently heat the remaining 50g sugar with 2 tablespoons water to dissolve. Bring to the boil then brush over the buns. Allow to cool before serving.

Per serving: 287 cals, 6g fat, 3.7g sat fat, 23.7g total sugars, trace salt

Mixed spice, nutmeg and orange give these buns a fabulous flavour

Serves 12
Prep time: 35 minutes,
plus cooling time
Cook time: 1 hour

Spooky spider cake

Celebrate Halloween with this devilishly good chocolate fudge cake

250g dark Belgian cooking chocolate
200g unsalted butter
200g light muscovado sugar
100ml soured cream
2 eggs, beaten
1 teaspoon vanilla extract
200g self-raising flour

5 tablespoons cocoa powder
250g golden icing sugar
8 Sainsbury's crunchy mint sticks
1 Sainsbury's basics mallow tea cake
1 piece Sainsbury's chocolate covered ginger
2 x writing icing pens, in black and white
green ribbon

1 Preheat the oven to 160°C, 140°C fan, gas 3. Line the base of a 20cm round cake tin with baking parchment. Over a low heat, melt 200g chocolate with the butter, muscovado sugar and 100ml hot water, stirring continuously. Remove from the heat and cool for 2–3 minutes.

2 Stir in the soured cream, eggs and vanilla extract. Sieve together the flour and cocoa powder, then whisk into the chocolate mixture. Pour into the cake tin. Bake in the oven for 50–60 minutes, or until a skewer inserted into the centre comes out clean. Leave to cool on a wire rack.

3 Place the icing sugar in a bowl. Add cold water, a little at a time, until the mixture is soft but spreadable. Invert the cake so you have a smooth surface for icing. Spread the icing over the top and allow it to dribble slightly over the edge.

4 Melt the remaining 50g chocolate, then allow to cool slightly to thicken. Spoon into a disposable piping bag. Snip off the end to give a very small hole and pipe a spider web, slightly off centre, on top of the cake.

5 Cut the mint sticks into 8 x 3cm pieces for the spider's upper legs and 8 x 2cm pieces for the lower legs. Using melted chocolate, join the upper legs to the lower legs and lay on their sides on baking parchment to set.

6 Place the tea cake on the web for the spider's body, and the chocolate ginger for the head. Using the writing icing pens, pipe on a pair of eyes. Arrange the legs and secure the ribbon around the base with a dot of icing.

Per serving: 537 cals, 26.3g fat, 16.1g sat fat, 55.3g total sugars, 0.3g salt

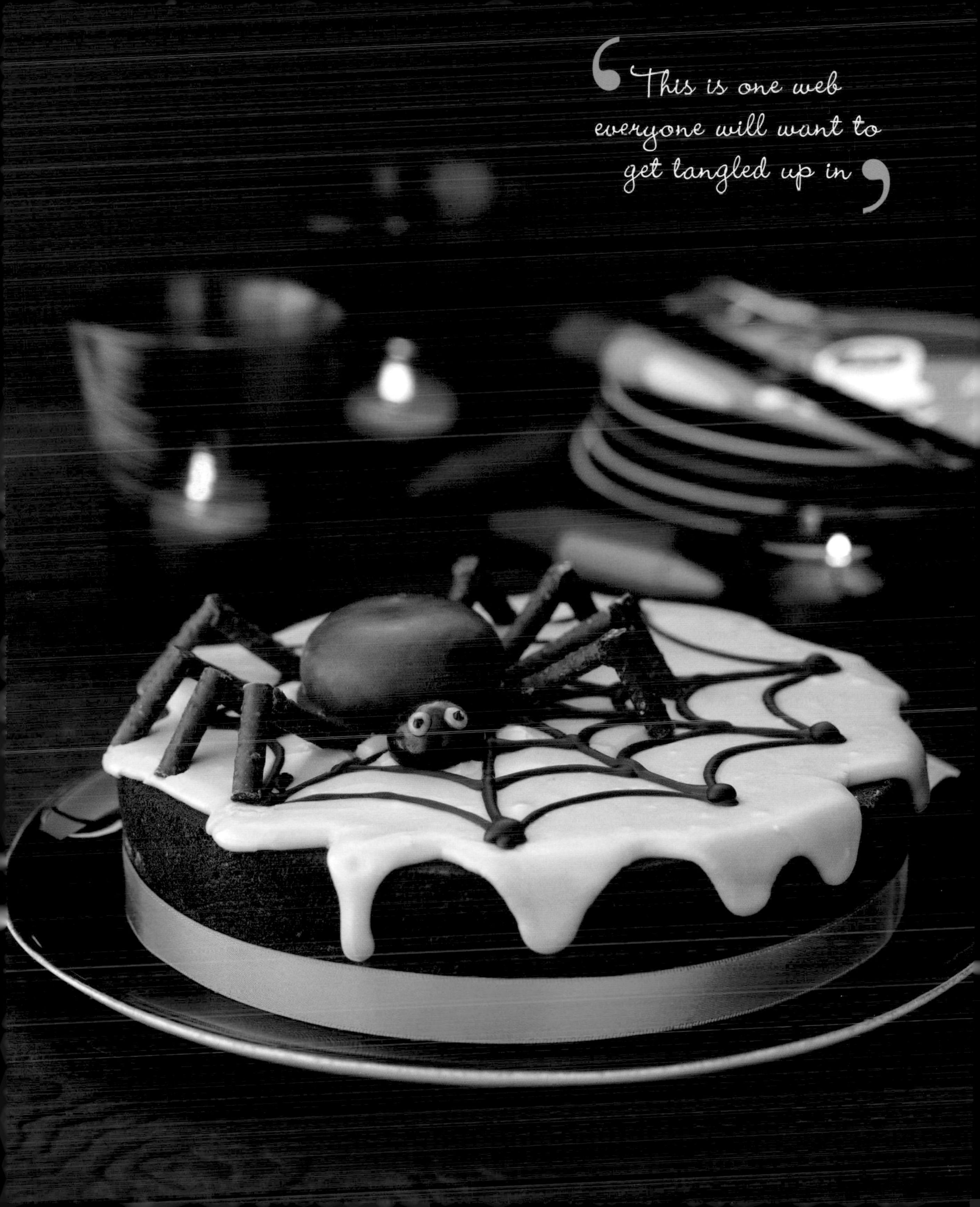

"This is one web everyone will want to get tangled up in"

Serves 10
Prep time: 45 minutes,
plus chilling time
Cook time: 20 minutes

Halloween graveyard traybake

Spooky gravestone biscuits, ghostly mice and jelly creepy crawlies make this traybake the perfect treat for Halloween

---

150g unsalted butter, softened
100g caster sugar
1 teaspoon vanilla extract
1 medium egg yolk, lightly beaten
200g plain flour, plus extra for dusting
200g Sainsbury's marshmallows, chopped
200g dark chocolate, broken up

1 x 4-pack Sainsbury's writing icing pens
1 x 300ml pot Sainsbury's double cream
3 teaspoons Sainsbury's pink glimmer sugar
2 Sainsbury's white mice
4 jelly fruit gums
sprigs of fresh mint

---

1 Using an electric hand mixer, cream 100g butter with the sugar and vanilla extract until well mixed and just creamy in texture. Do not over-mix or the cookies will spread during baking. Beat in the egg yolk until combined. Add the flour and mix on a low speed until a dough forms. Shape into a ball, wrap in clingfilm and chill in the fridge for at least 1 hour.

2 Preheat the oven to 190°C, fan 170°C, gas 5. Briefly knead the dough on a floured surface and roll to a thickness of 0.5cm. Cut out 18 'gravestones' measuring 4 x 6cm. Bake on a baking tray lined with baking parchment for 12–14 minutes, until golden brown at the edges. Cool on a wire rack.

3 Meanwhile, melt the marshmallows, the remaining 50g butter and the chocolate in a saucepan over a low heat. Set aside to cool slightly.

4 Using the writing icing pens, decorate 5 biscuits to look like gravestones. Crumble the remaining 13 biscuits by hand into chunky crumbs.

5 Whip the cream until thick. Fold through the cooled chocolate mixture along with the biscuit crumbs. Spoon into a 1.5-litre dish and scatter over the glimmer sugar. Arrange the mice and draw on eyes using the icing pens. Add the fruit gums and draw on legs to make them look like bugs. Chill for 1 hour. To serve, arrange the gravestones and poke sprigs of mint into the mousse.

Per serving: 589 cals, 35.6g fat, 22.6g sat fat, 39.3g total sugars, trace salt

Makes 22
Prep time: 25 minutes,
plus chilling time
Cook time: 12 minutes

Bonfire night firework cookies

Get the kids to help decorate these Catherine wheel and shooting star cookies to enjoy on Guy Fawkes Night

115g unsalted butter, softened
115g caster sugar
1 teaspoon ground ginger
1 tablespoon black treacle
1 medium egg, lightly beaten

300g plain flour, plus extra for dusting
50g stem ginger, finely chopped
1 x 4-pack Sainsbury's colour writing icing
pens (red, yellow, green and black)

1 Preheat the oven to 190°C, fan 170°C, gas 5. Line 2 baking trays with baking parchment.

2 In a bowl, beat together the butter, sugar and ginger until light and fluffy. Add the treacle and egg and whisk until combined, then beat in the flour and stem ginger. Chill in the fridge for 20 minutes.

3 On a floured surface, roll out the mixture to a thickness of 0.5cm. Using a 9cm round cutter, stamp out rounds for the Catherine wheels. Re-roll the excess dough and cut out shooting stars. Place on the baking trays and bake for 8-12 minutes, depending on size. The wheels should be ready before the shooting stars – just remove from the oven when the edges start to brown. Cool on a wire rack.

4 Use the coloured icing pens to decorate each biscuit as you like.

Per serving: 125 cals, 4.9g fat, 3.1g sat fat, 7.9g total sugars, trace salt

Makes 12
Prep time: 20 minutes,
plus chilling time
Cook time: 20 minutes

Mince pies

These classic Christmas favourites are easy to make and very moreish

---

175g plain flour, plus extra for dusting
100g unsalted butter
1 medium egg yolk, beaten

350g Taste the Difference mincemeat
icing sugar, for dusting

---

1 To make the pastry, rub the flour into the butter in a bowl. Make a well in the centre and add the egg yolk and 1 tablespoon cold water. Work into a dough, adding a drop more water if necessary. Knead gently, until smooth. Wrap in clingfilm and chill in the fridge for 15 minutes.

2 Preheat the oven to 200°C, fan 180°C, gas 6.

3 On a floured surface, roll out the pastry to a thickness of 0.5cm. Using a 7cm round cutter, stamp out 12 rounds. Line a 12-hole tart tin with the pastry rounds. Spoon a generous teaspoon of mincemeat into each case. Roll out the pastry trimmings and cut out small stars and trees and place on top of the mince pies.

4 Bake in the oven for 10 minutes. Reduce the oven temperature to 180°C, fan 160°C, gas 4 and bake for a further 8-10 minutes, until golden brown. Cool on a wire rack, then dust with icing sugar.

Per serving: 210 cals, 8.2g fat, 4.9g sat fat, 18.4g total sugars, trace salt

Serves 8
Prep time: 25 minutes,
plus overnight soaking
Cook time: 6–8 hours

Christmas pudding

You can make this traditional Christmas pud up to 2 months in advance

100g each raisins, currants and sultanas

75g ready-to-eat dried figs, chopped

50g candied peel, ½ chopped, ½ thinly sliced

1 teaspoon ground cinnamon

1 teaspoon mixed spice

½ teaspoon freshly ground nutmeg

200ml stout

2 tablespoons Amaretto liqueur

zest and juice of 1 orange

25g unsalted butter, plus extra for greasing

250g dark brown soft sugar

25g flaked almonds

50g pecan nuts

25g glacé cherries, chopped

100g vegetable suet

2 medium eggs, beaten

50g plain flour

100g breadcrumbs

1 Place the raisins, currants, sultanas, figs and chopped peel in a bowl with the cinnamon, mixed spice, nutmeg, stout, Amaretto and orange zest and juice. Mix well, cover and leave overnight in a cool place for the flavours to mature.

2 Heat the butter and 25g sugar in a pan until melted. Stir in the sliced peel, nuts and cherries, and arrange in the bottom of a greased 1.2-litre pudding basin.

3 Stir the suet, eggs, flour, breadcrumbs and remaining 225g sugar into the bowl of soaked dried fruit and mix well. Tip into the pudding basin and pack down tightly.

4 Prepare a large steamer or alternatively place a trivet or heatproof plate in a large pan with a lid. Cut 2 x 70cm lengths of baking parchment and a piece of extra wide foil (turkey foil is ideal). Place the baking parchment lengths on top of the foil, and place the pudding basin in the centre of the parchment. Wrap the pudding, with the foil on the outside. Secure with string, making a loop for easy removal.

5 Place the pudding in the steamer or pan. Add boiling water, filling halfway up the sides. Cover and steam for 6 hours, topping up the water regularly.

6 Remove the pudding from the steamer and discard the parchment and foil. Allow to cool, then re-wrap and store in a cool place for up to 2 months.

7 To reheat, steam for 2 hours or remove the foil and microwave for 5 minutes.

Per serving: 577 cals, 22.1g fat, 8.9g sat fat, 69.6g total sugars, 0.4g salt

"A festive centrepiece topped with almonds, pecans and glacé cherries"

Serves 24
Prep time: 30 minutes, plus 2-4 days' soaking
Cook time: 3½-4 hours

Christmas cake

A traditional, rich and fruity Christmas cake - see overleaf for how to ice it

400g currants
150g each raisins and sultanas
100g ready-to-eat, dried figs, chopped
100g ready-to-eat, dried prunes, chopped
100g glacé cherries, chopped
½ x 200g tub Sainsbury's cut mixed peel
100ml dark rum
50ml Grand Marnier
2 teaspoons mixed spice

zest of 1 lemon
zest and juice of 1 orange
2 teaspoons Taste the Difference Valencian orange essence
225g plain flour
225g salted butter, softened, plus extra for greasing
225g dark brown soft sugar
4 medium eggs

1 Place all the dried fruit, cherries, peel, alcohol, spice and zest in a large pan. Squeeze over the orange juice and bring to the boil. Tip into a large bowl and stir in the orange essence. Cool, then cover and set aside for 2-4 days (the longer it's left, the better the flavour), stirring daily.

2 When ready to bake, butter a 25cm springform round cake tin and line with 2 layers of baking parchment. To protect the cake during cooking, wrap the outside of the tin with a few sheets of brown paper and secure with string. Preheat the oven to 140°C, fan 120°C, gas 1.

3 Sift the flour twice into a large bowl. Place the butter and sugar in a different large bowl and beat with an electric hand mixer until light and fluffy. Beat in the eggs, one at a time, until combined. Fold the flour in gently with a large metal spoon, then fold in the soaked fruits. Spoon into the tin and level.

4 Cut a piece of brown paper to fit just over the cake and cut a 50p-sized hole in the centre. Place on the cake to prevent over-browning. Bake for 3½-4 hours, or until a skewer inserted into the cake comes out clean. Cool on a wire rack and store in an airtight container until ready to decorate.

Per serving: 285 cals, 9.1g fat, 5.5g sat fat, 38.1g total sugars, 0.3g salt

For a tasty fruit & nut topping
Brush the top of the cooled cake with 1 tablespoon melted apricot jam. Arrange Brazil nuts, walnuts, raisins, dried cranberries and dried dates, as desired, and coat with a further tablespoon of melted apricot jam to glaze

Decorates 1 cake
Prep time: 1 hour, plus
2–3 hours' setting time

How to decorate your Christmas cake

This icing on the cake really does make Christmas special

1 x 25cm Christmas cake (see previous page)
1 x 454g pack Sainsbury's white marzipan
3 tablespoons sieved apricot jam, warmed
1 tablespoon vodka, or water if preferred
750g Sainsbury's ready to roll white icing

a few drops each of red and green food colouring
250g fondant icing sugar
about 15 white sugar cubes
red ribbon

1   Place the cake on a flat serving plate. Roll out half the marzipan and cut to fit the top of the cake. Cut the remaining half into 1 or 2 strips to fit around the sides. Put the excess aside – you'll need about 60g marzipan later.

2   Brush the cake with the jam and place the marzipan around the sides and on the top. Brush the cake sparingly with the vodka or water. Roll out the icing into a circle large enough to drape over the cake and down the sides. Ease over the top of the cake and down the sides, pushing out any air bubbles as you go. Trim round the base with a knife and reserve the excess icing.

3   Colour about a quarter of the reserved marzipan with a few drops of red colouring and the remainder with green. Shape the red marzipan into small berries. Roll out the green marzipan and cut out small holly leaves. Roll out the excess white icing and cut out large holly leaves. Using a knife, lightly score each leaf down the centre. Place the white leaves over a roll of foil to make them curl and leave to firm up for 2–3 hours.

4   Put the fondant icing sugar in a bowl and stir in drops of water until the mixture is just soft enough to slowly fall from a spoon. Using a teaspoon or a piping bag, spread the icing around the outside edge of the cake and allow it to slowly drip down the side. Arrange the holly leaves and berries on top. Lightly crush the sugar cubes in a bowl. Sprinkle over the top to make the cake sparkle. Secure the ribbon around the base with a dot of the fondant icing.

Per serving: 552 cals, 13.7g fat, 6.3g sat fat, 92.6g total sugars, 0.4g salt

Makes 1 loaf (8 slices)
Prep time: 45 minutes,
plus proving time
Cook time: 30 minutes

Stollen

This marzipan-filled festive favourite will delight your Christmas guests

175g Sainsbury's mixed dried fruit

75g glacé cherries, quartered

50g shelled pistachio nuts, chopped

5 cardamom pods, seeds removed and crushed

½ tablespoon vanilla extract

zest of 2 unwaxed lemons

375g strong white bread flour, plus
extra for dusting

7g sachet fast action dried yeast

50g caster sugar

50g unsalted butter, plus extra for greasing
and 2 tablespoons melted butter

150ml milk

1 large egg, beaten

175g white marzipan

icing sugar, to dust

1 Place the mixed fruit in a bowl with the cherries, pistachios, cardamom,
   vanilla extract and lemon zest. Cover and set aside.

2 Tip the flour, yeast and caster sugar into a mixing bowl. Over a low heat,
   melt 50g butter, then pour in the milk and allow to warm. Stir in the egg.
   Pour the milk into the flour mixture and combine to form a soft dough.

3 Tip out onto a floured surface and knead for 10 minutes, until smooth and
   elastic. Place in a lightly oiled bowl. Cover with clingfilm and leave in a
   warm place to rise until the dough has doubled in size (about 1-1¼ hours).

4 Roll out the dough on a floured surface, then knead in the fruit mixture.
   Cover with oiled clingfilm and leave to rest in a warm place for 20 minutes.

5 Preheat the oven to 190°C, fan 170°C, gas 5. Lightly grease a baking tray.
   Shape the marzipan into a log, about 3cm thick, and set aside. Roll out
   the dough to a 30 x 20cm rectangle, and place the marzipan log on top.
   Fold up the dough, sealing the marzipan inside. Transfer to the baking tray.
   Cover with lightly oiled clingfilm and leave in a warm place for 30 minutes.

6 Bake for 25-30 minutes, or until risen and pale golden. Remove from the
   oven and brush with 2 tablespoons melted butter. Cool on a wire rack,
   then dust generously with icing sugar to serve.

Per slice: 523 cals, 16.4g fat, 6.1g sat fat, 46.4g total sugars, 0.1g salt

A fruity and spicy festive treat, filled with scrummy marzipan

Makes 30
Prep time: 20 minutes,
plus chilling time
Cook time: 10 minutes

Stained-glass cookies

Kids will revel in making these biscuits to hang on the Christmas tree

175g unsalted butter, softened
200g caster sugar
1 medium egg
1 teaspoon vanilla extract

400g plain flour, plus extra for dusting
1 x 250g bag Sainsbury's clear fruits (boiled sweets)
coloured ribbon, for hanging biscuits on tree

1 Preheat the oven to 180°C, fan 160°C, gas 4. Line 2 baking trays with baking parchment.

2 Using an electric hand mixer, beat the butter and sugar together in a large bowl until pale and fluffy. Beat in the egg and add the vanilla extract.

3 Fold in the flour and stir until combined. You may need to add a little extra if the mixture is too sticky, but don't over-mix or the dough will be tough.

4 Halve the dough and roll into 2 flat discs. Wrap in clingfilm and chill in the fridge for 1 hour.

5 On a surface dusted with flour, roll out the pastry to a thickness of 0.5cm. Using a 10cm star-shaped cutter, cut out stars and place on the baking trays.

6 Stamp out a small hole in the middle of each star, the same size as the boiled sweets. Place one sweet into each hole. Using a skewer, make a small hole in the top of each star (to hang the stars on the tree later). Bake for 8-10 minutes, or until turning golden. Cool on a wire rack.

7 If hanging your biscuits, thread some ribbon through the hole in each biscuit and tie a knot in the end. Keep in an airtight container until needed.

Per serving: 151 cals, 5.2g fat, 3.2g sat fat, 14g total sugars, trace salt

‘Get kids involved in the festive fun with these jewel-like, easy-to-make biscuits’

10 top baking tips for great results

1 Preheat the oven to the required temperature for at least 15 minutes before you use it, and try not to open the door too often because it changes the internal temperature and affects air flow.

2 Chill shortcrust pastry in the fridge for at least 15 minutes before rolling out and for a further 15 minutes before baking. This relaxes the pastry and prevents shrinkage during cooking.

3 When working with pastry try to stand in a cool area of your kitchen, as the fat will begin to melt if it becomes too hot.

4 Use medium-sized free-range eggs unless otherwise stated. Remove from the fridge about 2 hours before using, as cold eggs can cause the mixture to curdle, resulting in a flat cake.

5 Always measure ingredients carefully and use weighing scales if possible. Precision is essential for achieving good results from baking recipes.

6 An oven will often have a 'hot patch' so turn your biscuits or cake around halfway through baking to ensure even cooking and a lovely golden colour.

7 When baking a cake, work as quickly as you can once you've added the wet ingredients to the dry ingredients, as the raising agents start to work pretty much immediately.

8 Blind baking pastry is essential if using an uncooked filling or a filling that takes less time to cook than the case. Line pastry with baking parchment, top with baking beans (see tip 9) and cook before adding your filling and baking again, if required.

9 Don't have ceramic baking beans? Use uncooked haricot beans or rice instead. Pack them against the sides to prevent pastry from shrinking.

10 Bake on the middle shelf of your oven so that air circulates around your cake.

Index

Conversion table

Weights		Volume		Measurements		Oven temperatures		fan	gas
15g	½ oz	25ml	1fl oz	2mm	¹⁄₁₆ in	110°C	90°C		
25g	1oz	50ml	2fl oz	3mm	⅛ in	120°C	100°C		½
40g	1½ oz	75ml	3fl oz	4mm	⅙ in	140°C	120°C		1
50g	2 oz	100ml	4fl oz	5mm	¼ in	150°C	130°C		2
60g	2½ oz	150ml	5fl oz (¼ pint)	1cm	½ in	160°C	140°C		3
75g	3 oz	175ml	6fl oz	2cm	¾ in	180°C	160°C		4
100g	3½ oz	200ml	7fl oz	2.5cm	1in	190°C	170°C		5
125g	4 oz	225ml	8fl oz	3cm	1¼ in	200°C	180°C		6
150g	5 oz	250ml	9fl oz	4cm	1½ in	220°C	200°C		7
175g	6 oz	300ml	10fl oz (½ pint)	4.5cm	1¾ in	230°C	210°C		8
200g	7 oz	350ml	13fl oz	5cm	2 in	240°C	220°C		9
225g	8 oz	400ml	14fl oz	6cm	2½ in				
250g	9 oz	450ml	16fl oz (¾ pint)	7.5cm	3 in				
275g	10 oz	600ml	20fl oz (1 pint)	9cm	3½ in				
300g	11 oz	750ml	25fl oz (1¼ pints)	10cm	4 in				
350g	12 oz	900ml	30fl oz (1½ pints)	13cm	5 in				
375g	13 oz	1 litre	34fl oz (1¾ pints)	13.5cm	5¼ in				
400g	14 oz	1.2 litres	40fl oz (2 pints)	15cm	6 in				
425g	15 oz	1.5 litres	52fl oz (2½ pints)	16cm	6½ in				
450g	1lb	1.8 litres	60fl oz (3 pints)	18cm	7in				
500g	1lb 2 oz			19cm	7½ in				
650g	1lb 7 oz			20cm	8in				
675g	1½ lb			23cm	9in				
700g	1lb 9 oz			24cm	9½ in				
750g	1lb 11 oz			25.5cm	10 in				
900g	2lb			28cm	11 in				
1kg	2lb 4 oz			30cm	12 in				
1.5kg	3lb 6 oz			32.5cm	13 in				
				35cm	14 in				

Kids

Look out for this handprint - the kids can help make these recipes

Gluten-free

The following recipes are ideal if you're following a gluten-free diet

Credits

Food
Senior food editor Georgina Fuggle
Food assistant Mima Sinclair
Food assistant Hannah Yeadon

Design
Senior art director David Jenkins
Designer Nina Brennan
Stylist Morag Farquhar

Editorial
Editor Jo Clifton
Sub-editor Samantha Jones

Account management
Senior account director Lynne de Lacy
Account manager Lucy Rainer
Account executive Amy Fixter
Publishing director Dorcas Jamieson

Photography
Dan Jones, Gareth Morgans

Print & production
Production manager Mike Lamb
Colour origination F1 Colour Ltd
Printers Butler, Tanner and
Dennis Ltd, Frome and London

Special thanks to...
Valerie Barrett, Sal Henley, Sonja Edridge,
Elaine Gowran, Nicky Gyopari,
Sam Stowell, Patricia Baker

MIX
Paper from
responsible sources
FSC® C023561